German Half-Tracked Vehicles of World War 2

German Half-Tracked Vehicles of World War 2

Unarmoured support vehicles of the German Army 1933/45

John Milsom

London: Arms & Armour Press

New York: Hippocrene Books, Inc

Published in 1975
in Great Britain by
Arms and Armour Press
Lionel Leventhal Limited
2–6 Hampstead High Street
London NW3 1PR

SBN 85368 330 1

Published in 1975
in the United States by
Hippocrene Books, Inc.
171 Madison Avenue,
New York, N.Y. 10016.

ISBN 0-88254-354-7
Library of Congress Catalog
Card Number 75 - 12783

Printed by T. & A. Constable Limited, Edinburgh, Scotland.

Contents

Introduction

As far as the Wehrmacht period is concerned, the provision of military transport vehicles to the German armed forces began with the introduction of the re-armament programme in 1932. There was, however, a great deal of earlier work in this field, that greatly contributed to the final selection of vehicle types.

Over the period 1927–8 the General Staff introduced the Kraftfahrrüstungsprogramm (the Motorisation Programme), with which they attempted to lay down the specifications and requirements for military automotive equipment. The Programme was finalised during 1929.

When Hitler came to power in 1933, a great impetus was given to military motorisation in Germany and efforts were made to mould industry into an organisation more suited to fulfilling military requirements. With the foundation of the new Wehrmacht, attempts were made to standardise vehicle types adopted by the army. For specially-designed military vehicles a new system of numbering was introduced, and these Sd.Kfz. (Sönder-kraftfahrzeug) numbers were allocated to vehicles to denote their tactical or military function irrespective of make or model.

Prior to the outbreak of World War Two, an officer named von Schell introduced a standardisation programme for the armed forces whereby select commercial and specially-developed automotive equipment was categorised. Under this programme, efforts were made to reduce the variety of existing types to a bare minimum. Half-track tractors had proved extremely popular with the army and the Luftwaffe and their production was therefore continued. Eight models of half-track were kept in production—including the motor-cycle tractor and two Maultier (mule) vehicles, as follows:

Motor-cycle tractor Sd.Kfz.2. Used by despatch riders, infantry, harassing detachments, etc, for anti-tank and mountain guns, and for ammunition supplies and weapons in special trailers.
2-ton Maultier vehicle. Replaced the medium cross-country lorry for armoured and motorised units and could also act as substitute for 1-ton and 3-ton semi-tracked tractors.

4½-ton Maultier vehicle. Substitute for 5-ton semi-tracked tractor, which was no longer being produced. It was used for towing the 8.8cm Pak 43.
1-ton semi-tracked tractor. For towing 3.7cm Pak 36 and 5cm Pak 38, and as an SP mounting for the 2cm Flak 30.
3-ton semi-tracked tractor. For towing 7.5cm Pak 40 and Pak 41, 15cm s.I.G.33 or 10.5cm le.F.H.18.
8-ton semi-tracked tractor. For towing 8.8cm Flak, 10cm K.18, 15cm s.F.H.18 and as an SP mounting for 3.7cm Flak and 2cm Flakvierling. Also used as bridging vehicle.
12-ton semi-tracked tractor. For towing 10.5cm Flak, 17cm K in Mrs. Laf. and 21cm Mörser 18 (both in two separate loads), 15cm K.18 and 16. Could be used as a tank-towing vehicle.
18-ton semi-tracked tractor. For towing 35.5cm Mörser (7 separate loads) and 24cm K3 (5 separate loads), carrying mobile crane (6-ton or 10-ton) or as tank-towing vehicle.

The Germans also made a considerable attempt to obtain production of complete half-tracked vehicles, parts for assembly into new half-tracks and spare parts for these vehicles by a number of firms dispersed throughout France. The major firms involved were Peugeot, Renault, Lorraine, Panhard and Simca.

Extensive use was made by the Luftwaffe and the Wehrmacht of captured French semi-tracked vehicles (produced by SOMUA, Unic, Panhard and Citröen), but these are not dealt with in this volume.

The First Generation of Half-Tracked Vehicles (Zugkraftwagen)

Much use was made in the German Army of 'Zugkraftwagen' (Zg.Kw), or towing tractors, with one or more steered wheels at the front and a tracked suspension system at the rear. These were classified not by load-carrying capacity but by trailer load and would be referred to either by this means or by their special vehicle number (Sd.Kfz.Nr.). As distinct from the Maultier (mule) vehicles, which were purely load-carriers, these were solely for towing. The adoption of this type of vehicle followed experience gained during World War One with Daimler-Benz 'Marienwagens' and 'Kraft-Protze'.

The design of German half-tracked (strictly speaking three-quarters-tracked) vehicles commenced during 1926 to fulfil a requirement for motorising the artillery arm. Pursuance of this form of vehicle has been attributed to the personal endeavours of Ernst Kniepkamp (head of the Heereswaffenamt, who was also attributed with the successful adoption of overlapping wheel arrangements). During 1928, Krauss-Maffei AG tested a prototype MS 4-wheeled tractor with tracks in place of the rear wheels. This was a dual purpose vehicle in that the tracks could be removed for road driving. The adoption of the semi-tracked configuration resulted from a series of extensive trials. Richard Student wrote[1]: ". . . Development of the half-tracked tractor in Germany evolved from studies with the conventional full-tracked type. Following trials with rubber-band tracks, German engineers came to the conclusion that only a steel-type track could meet the demands for durability and long life and lend itself adequately to the replacement of damaged parts. After extensive proving and research, a tracked running gear was evolved which answered all the demands. Its basic characteristics were: (a) Lubricated bearings in the track links; (b) Rubber pads to dampen noise; (c) Large wheels with rubber tyres, and a front-located sprocket. This track system permitted high speeds with relatively low power. The degree of sensitivity in the steering system required for road travel could not, however, be obtained by track braking. In order to compensate for this, the vehicles were provided with additional front wheels which were used only for steering through slight angles (and thereby at high speeds); and for greater steering angles, operation of the steering wheel brought into play the steering brakes of the track system. It is considered that the use of lubricated steel tracks enabled the prolonged towing of heavy loads . . ."

During 1932, a standardised family of semi-tracked vehicles was scheduled for production under the control of Wa.Prüf.6 (Heereswäffenamt Branch 6), embracing a wide range of towing capacities. At first the army requested three basic classes—light, medium and heavy; but these designations were later modified and vehicles were classified according to their trailer capacity. The light class became the 5-ton, the medium the 8-ton, and the heavy the 12-ton class; during 1934 a parent firm was selected to conduct the design and development work for each weight class. At this time, two further vehicles were ordered—the 3-ton class and the 1-ton class; and during 1936 the last class (18-ton) was ordered. Other firms were requested to assist in production whenever necessary.

In order to maintain interchangeability of parts, the authorities refrained from introducing new models. It is interesting to note that the models with which the Wehrmacht and the Luftwaffe were equipped prior to World War Two appeared in service in the following order:

8-ton Sd.Kfz.7. Medium semi-tracked tractor (m.Zg.Kw.) 8-ton, developed by Krauss-Maffei AG, München.

5-ton Sd.Kfz.6. Medium semi-tracked tractor (m.Zg.Kw.) 5-ton, developed by Büssing NAG, Berlin Oberschön-weide.

12-ton Sd.Kfz.8. Heavy semi-tracked tractor (s.Zg.Kw.) 12-ton, developed by Daimler-Benz AG, Berlin Marien-felde.

1. "Das Halbkettenfahrzeug als militärisches Zugmittel", by von Dipl. Ing. Richard Student, VDI, *Wehrtechnische Monatshefte*, No. 8, August 1939.

3-ton Sd.Kfz.11. Light semi-tracked tractor (le.Zg.Kw.) 3-ton, developed by Borgward (formerly Hansa-Lloyd-Goliath AG), Bremen.

1-ton Sd.Kfz.10. Light semi-tracked tractor (le.Zg.Kw.) 1-ton, developed by Demag, Wetter/Ruhr.

18-ton Sd.Kfz.9. Heavy semi-tracked tractor (s.Zg.Kw.) 18-ton, developed by Famo, Breslau.

Each firm was responsible for the development and production of pilot vehicles for its particular class. Subsequently, as already mentioned, other concerns were obliged to build its model(s).

A certain level of standardisation was achieved in that all models were powered by Maybach engines (either 6- or 12-cylinder, water-cooled).

The first one or two capital letters of a semi-track designation signified the firm originally making the vehicle, as follows:

D—Demag;
HL—Hansa-Lloyd (later Borgward);
H—Hanomag;
KM—Krauss-Maffei;
BN—Büssing·NAG;
DB—Daimler-Benz;
F—Famo.

Since the types developed by these manufacturers were made later by a number of other firms, however, the mark type is not a reliable guide to the original manufacturer—whose name could nevertheless be found on the vehicle name-plate.

The very early models were noted for their extremely short track sections (half-tracks), but later models had the track section lengthened to improve cross-country performance (three-quarter-tracks). The earlier models also had leaf-spring suspension; but some of the later versions adopted torsion bars carrying cranked carrier arms. All models in the 1- and 3-ton classes had this type of suspension.

The semi-tracks were designed so that the sides of the body were sufficiently high to obscure seated personnel to shoulder height. With all inspection hatches of the hull closed, the main body of the vehicle was practically watertight when traversing deep water.

Development of this first generation of semi-tracks reached a satisfactory conclusion by 1939, the models then in production being continued throughout the war with only minor modification (with the exception of the 5-ton model, which was eventually superseded by the S.WS). Some of these vehicles were supplemented by Maultier (mule) vehicles (see page 79).

Automotive characteristics of the early semi-tracked vehicles

Chassis. The chassis frame was of welded construction and consisted of two side-members braced by cross-members at the front—forming the mounting bracket for the front mudguards—under, and supporting, the engine at the extreme rear. Tubular members, enclosing the torsion-bar suspension of the bogie and idler wheels, also crossed the side-members and assisted load distribution. Petrol tanks, compressed-air cylinders for the braking system and, in the case of the larger vehicles, a winch were held within the chassis frame. Frame-type chassis were used in the heavier models, hull-type construction in the lighter ones.

Power Unit. Maybach water-cooled petrol engines were used, ranging from a straight six of about 4,000cc (in the Zg.Kw.8t) to a V12 of over 10,000cc. Equipment fitted included Bosch electric and inertia starters, magnetos and air-compressors, Pallas petrol pumps and Solex twin down-draught carburettors. The engine compartment layout followed normal wheeled vehicle practice.

Transmission. Transmission was through a twin-plate multiple-sprung dry clutch mounted on the engine flywheel, and either a Variorex semi-automatic (pre-selector) gearbox, having seven forward speeds or, in some cases (e.g. the Zg.Kw.3t), an ordinary type of gearbox having four forward speeds and one reverse speed. In the Variorex gearbox an auxiliary lever had two steps, forward and reverse, and in a later position, three low gears could be engaged for reversing. With the ordinary gearbox, an auxiliary box provided high and low ratios for road and cross-country running.

Differential. The differential was of the Cletrac controlled type incorporating two internal-expanding brakes, one for each track. The driving sprockets for the tracks were at the front.

Sprockets. From the steering brakes the drive passed through two couplings to the final reduction gears, and thence to the sprockets. These were fully floating, and each consisted of two narrow solid rubber-tyred wheels to which were fitted steel rollers serving as normal teeth (twelve roller teeth on the Zg.Kw.1t and fourteen on the heavier models.) An internal expanding brake, foot-operated and compressed-air assisted, was mounted inside each sprocket. Some of the later models had modified tank-type sprockets, the tracks also being modified.

Steering. Rotation of the steering wheel from 0° to 15° either side of straight did not bring track steering into operation. Rotation beyond 15° initiated the operation of steering brakes on the appropriate track. These brakes were brought into play by a drop-arm on the steering box, connected to a rod moving two levers connected to a cross-tube. From these two levers cables operated the steering brakes. An indicator, fitted to the steering column, showed the direction in which the front wheels were pointing.

Suspension. The front wheels, fitted with tyres of pneumatic or 'run-flat' type, were mounted on a tubular axle and sprung by a single transverse semi-elliptic spring mounted at the centre in a swinging cradle. Two shock-absorbers (Luvac type) were fitted, and the upward movement of the axle on either side was limited by rubber stops fitted on the chassis. The front axle was retained by radius rods anchoring it to the main chassis cross-brace. Exceptions were the early 1-ton series—models D11 1, D11 2 and D11 3—which had centre-wheel pivoting axles and various arrangements of the torsion-bar springing.

Track Assembly. Each side consisted of a driving sprocket, a number of equal-size double-rimmed bogie wheels and an idler wheel, all mounted in a train. Of the bogie wheels, the odd numbers (counting from the front) had their rims set close together and the even numbers had their rims set wide apart. This allowed the narrower wheels to run between the wider rims, the wheels being set rim-to-axle. The idler wheel was adjustable, so providing the means of controlling the tension of the tracks. The sprocket had a fixed mounting.

Two types of suspension system were employed. In the earlier models, the bogie wheels were mounted in threes—two adjacent wheels on a forked axle and the third on a straight stub-axle. Both axles were then sprung by a semi-elliptic spring. This type of suspension was later superseded by one in which each bogie wheel was mounted on a trailing crank-arm and sprung by a torsion-bar anchored in the opposite side of the chassis. The torsion-bars of the corresponding wheels of each track were mounted one above the other or side by side in a tubular chassis member. The upward movement of the crank-arms was limited by stops mounted on the chassis side-members. The idler wheels were fitted with Luvac type shock-absorbers.

Tracks. These were made up of hinged metal track plates, each of which had a rubber insert retained by four studs—so that the inserts were easily removable. Each plate had a small tongue inside, which passed between the rims of the bogie wheels. Small grip chains were provided for fitting to every third insert when traversing particularly difficult terrain. A very characteristic type of track was used, having detachable rubber pads and sealed lubricated needle-roller bearings for the track pins—the latter feature ensuring low rolling resistance, long track life and constant pitch.

Brakes. The foot-brake pedal was connected to an internal expanding brake mounted inside each sprocket; and the hand brake was connected to the steering brakes, applying both simultaneously. All brakes were assisted by compressed-air, supplied from cylinders mounted on the chassis frame, and a Bosch compressor driven by the engine. Brakes were not normally fitted to the front wheels. In the later models Argus disc brakes were used.

Bodywork of the early semi-tracked vehicles

Zg.Kw. 1-ton. This vehicle was essentially a troop-carrier, accommodation for a crew of eight (plus the driver) being provided in the well of the body. No doors were provided, the crew simply clambering over the sides to mount and dismount. A windscreen and a canvas hood, which could be drawn forward to cover both the top and sides, were fitted. The track guards were square with bevelled ends, and the body sides were low over the track guards.

Zg.Kw. 3-ton. The 3-ton vehicle differed from the Zg.Kw. 1-ton in that the body was built on more conventional lorry lines. There was a separate driver's cab, and the front and rear mudguards formed a continuous pressing. The body and frame were constructed of electrically-welded sheet metal.

Zg.Kw. 5-ton to Zg.Kw. 18-ton. These were all built on the same lines and were provided with two or three rows of seats at the front for the crew, behind which was a locker for equipment or ammunition. Weather flaps were provided. There was no separate driver's cab, the driver occupying the left-hand seat of the front row. Apart from considerations of size, there was little to

differentiate the 5- and 8-ton models. The 12-ton model was similar to the 8-ton but for a distinct hump at the front of the track guard where it cleared the sprocket. In the 18-ton vehicle there were only two rows of seats, including that for the driver and behind these was a larger load space. The mudguard and track guard formed a continuous pressing, with a depression and footstep between the two.

The various models could be identified by the number and shape of the holes in the bogie wheels as shown in the following diagram:

MOTOR-CYCLE TRACTOR (HK-100) SERIES	6 HOLES
1-TON TRACTOR (Sd.Kfz.10) SERIES	5 HOLES
3-TON TRACTOR (Sd.Kfz.11) SERIES	8 HOLES
5-TON TRACTOR (Sd.Kfz.6) SERIES	8 HOLES
8-TON TRACTOR (Sd.Kfz.7) SERIES	7 HOLES (8 on early models)
12-TON TRACTOR (Sd.Kfz.8) SERIES	8 HOLES
18-TON TRACTOR (Sd.Kfz.9) SERIES	8 HOLES

A leading engineer concerned with the development of German semi-tracked vehicles stated that, in his opinion, 'all German semi-tracks tended to be overloaded and, as a result, suspension failures were frequent'; for this reason, the bogie wheels on the 3-ton model were stiffened by pressing the form of spokes in them and also actually welding reinforcing spokes on the inner wheels. Gearboxes were, he recorded, satisfactory but difficult to manufacture. As far as was possible, common components were used in the design of the 3-, 5- and 8-ton vehicles—the difficulty in manufacture being mainly due to the large number of different surfaces that required machining. The engineer further stated that engines were not as reliable as they should have been, as too little time had been spent upon them. They were brought into general service within a very short time of the production of prototypes.

Leichter Zugkraftwagen 1-ton Sd.Kfz.10

Following an official military requirement for a 1-ton semi-tracked tractor, Demag of Wetter/Ruhr commenced development during 1932. The vehicle was required to operate as a troop carrier and also as a tractor for light artillery and supply trailers (Sd.Ah.32). It was mainly used to tow 37mm and 50mm anti-tank guns,

75mm and 150mm infantry howitzers and 20mm anti-aircraft guns.

The first experimental vehicle of the series, D11 1, appeared during the first half of 1934. Further development resulted in two more trial vehicles—the D11 2 and the D11 3. The essential changes made in these models was the successive lengthening of the track system in order to stabilise the vehicle across country. The D11 1 started with three bogie wheels per side, the D11 2 had four, and the D11 3 had five. These prototypes had bullet-proof tyres. By 1937 a pre-production model D6 was completed; and eventually, during 1939, there appeared the D7, which was standardised for service use as the Sd.Kfz.10. Production of this model continued until 1944 and about 25,000 were produced, excluding some 7,500 chassis used for the armoured Sd.Kfz.250 series.

Although Demag initiated the series and undertook early production, the main manufacturers of these vehicles were Mechanische Werke Cottbus in Silesia and the Saurer Werke in Vienna. The reason for this was that Demag was using its productive capacity to the full to turn out chassis for the armoured version Sd.Kfz.50. French manufacturers such as Lorraine, Panhard, Peugeot, Renault and Simca were also drawn into the programme. And some vehicles were produced by Adler, Büssing NAG and MIAG: Büssing NAG and Adler produced 4,500 and 5,360 respectively, excluding some 7,500 chassis used for armoured versions.

Chronological development was as follows:

1934 Demag D11 1 was the first prototype in the series and it weighed 4 tons. It had a crew of two men, was powered by a BMW-315 6-cylinder engine developing 28hp, had a ZF gearbox, hydraulic brakes, and torsion-bar suspension on both wheels and tracks. There were three bogie wheels per side.

1934 Demag D11 2 was the second prototype. Weighing 2½ tons, it was similar to D11 1 but had an extra bogie wheel on each side (total, four).

1936 Demag D11 3 was the third prototype. Weighing 3½ tons, it carried four men in addition to a two-man crew. It was powered by a new BMW-319 6-cylinder engine, developing 42hp. Provided with an extra bogie wheel on each side (total, five), it was otherwise similar to the previous models.

1936 Demag D4 was a project design only. It was to have been fitted with a Maybach 4-cylinder 65hp HL25 engine, and was to have had transverse leaf suspension on the front wheels. Otherwise, it was to have been similar to the D11 3.

1937 Demag D6 was a 4-ton pre-production vehicle built between 1937 and 1938. It was powered by the Maybach NL38 TRKM 6-cylinder in-line OHV engine of 3.79 litres capacity with an output of 83hp at 2,400rpm, and it had a Demag-Adler gearbox. Otherwise, it was similar to the previous model.

1939 Demag D7 was the final production machine, standardised as Sd.Kfz.10. Production began in 1939 and ended in 1944. Powered by a Maybach HL42 6-cylinder 100hp engine, the vehicle had a Maybach Variorex model SRG 10218H pre-selective gearbox. Otherwise, it was similar to the previous model.

1939 Demag D8 was a project design only. It was to have had one extra bogie wheel per side (total, six) and a new gearbox—model VG 102128H—with an extra gear ratio to give a higher maximum speed. Otherwise, it was to have been similar to the previous machine. Work on it was terminated because of the success of the D7.

1939 Sd.Kfz.10/1 was a specially-adapted light gas-detector vehicle (designated Leichter Gasspührkraftwagen) based on the D7 model but with seating arrangements for eight men (see Appendix 1).

1939 Sd.Kfz.10/2 was a specially-adapted light decontamination vehicle (designated Leichter Entgiftungskraftwagen) based on the D7 model but with seating arrangements for four men, racks for eight drums of lime, and a spreader-hopper at the rear (see Appendix 1).

1939 Sd.Kfz.10/3 was a specially-adapted light-bulk contamination vehicle (designated Leichter Spruhkraftwagen) based on the D7 model but with a spraying unit fed from a large storage tank. The original two-man crew was retained, and the vehicle was used for spraying blister gas (see Appendix 1).

Production of the Sd.Kfz.10:

1940	*1941*	*1942*	*1943*	*1944*
3,096	?	2,868	2,724	873

Leichter Zugkraftwagen 3-ton Sd.Kfz.11

Development of this vehicle was initiated during 1934 under the sponsorship of Hansa-Lloyd-Goliath (later Borgward) AG in Bremen. In that year the first model appeared and was designated HL kl 2. Shortly after this, during 1935, the HL kl 3 was produced. An attempt was then made to transfer the engine to the end of the vehicle so as to facilitate the application of an armoured body, and in this form the vehicle was designated the HL kl 3(H). During 1938 developmental responsibility for this series was transferred to Hanomag of Hanover, who subsequently became the parent firm for the entire 3-ton semi-track series. The final version was produced during 1939 and standardised as the Sd.Kfz.11. Hansa-Lloyd became Borgward during this year.

The Sd.Kfz.11 was eventually produced by Hanomag of Hannover-Linden, Borgward of Bremen, Auto-Union AG of Frankfurt, Adler (from 1942–45), Horch AG of Zwickau, and Skoda of Prague. In France, Delahaye was intended to participate in the production programme during 1942 but no vehicles were ever delivered. A total of over 25,000 of this type, excluding 16,000 armoured versions, were produced.

The vehicle was employed initially to tow the 105mm howitzer or an ammunition trailer, and was also used for drawing 75mm and 88mm anti-tank guns. Some vehicles were used by chemical warfare units. Nebelwerfer units, in particular, used the 3-ton vehicle to tow rocket launchers and to carry ammunition—in which role it was fitted with special ammunition racks.

Towards the end of the war, some vehicles received a wooden load platform and had their fuel capacity increased to 160 litres to fulfil the role of long-range logistic vehicles. Others were fitted as ambulances.

As a result of the retreat of the German Army in Russia, the manufacture of 3-ton semi-tracked vehicles, and Tiger and Panther tanks, was officially stated to be of the highest priority.

Chronological development was as follows

1934 Hansa-Lloyd-Goliath HL kl 2 was the first prototype for the 3-ton class. It weighed 5 tons, had a crew of eight men and was powered by a Borgward Type 3500 70hp 6-cylinder engine. It had a Borgward 4-speed gearbox, and mechanical road and steering brakes. Suspension on the wheels was by leaf springs, and on the tracks by torsion-bar (four bogie wheels per side).

1935 Borgward HL kl 3(H). This vehicle had the engine moved to the rear to enable the application of an armoured body, which was never fitted.

1935 Borgward HL kl 3. This was very similar in appearance to the HL kl 2, but the engine covers and radiator were more like those of the production model. Although it employed the same engine, there was a ZF gearbox with five forward speeds instead of four.

1936 Borgward HL kl 4(H) had a new Borgward 100hp 6-cylinder engine but used the original Borgward gearbox. The suspension had two extra bogie wheels per side (total, 6). The engine was at the rear, and the vehicle was intended to have been armoured and armed.

1936 Borgward HL kl 5 was a 7-ton pre-production machine powered by a Borgward 70hp L3500L 6-cylinder engine. Otherwise, it was similar to the previous model. In all, 505 were built.

1937 Borgward HL kl 6 was a production model standardised as Leichter Zugkraftwagen 3t Sd.Kfz.11. Development and production was taken over by Hanomag and Adler, their models both being called H kl 6. It had a crew of nine men and weighed 7.2 tons. This vehicle was initially powered by a Maybach HL38 engine, which was subsequently replaced by a Maybach HL42 6-cylinder engine developing 110hp. It also had a Hanomag gearbox but was otherwise similar to the previous model. In all, 2,067 were built by Borgward and 4,300 were built by Adler. Hanomag produced 6,270 (excluding 16,000 armoured versions). These vehicles were also built by Auto-Union (Werke Horch) and Skoda in Prague.

1938 Hanomag H8(H) differed in having a Variorex gearbox. Only one prototype was built, with the engine mounted at the rear to cater for an armoured body.

1939 Hanomag H7 was an experimental model with Maybach pre-selective gearbox, hydraulic steering brakes and pneumatic road brakes. It was otherwise similar to the H kl 6. Under the von Schell Programme, it was intended to be a standard 3-ton vehicle (Einheitsfahrzeug) to replace all previous models, but no further development work took place.

1939 H kl 6n; Sd.Kfz.11/1 Nebelkraftwagen. This was a smoke vehicle carrying racks of smoke generators. It was also used to carry ammunition and to act as a tractor for the Nebelwerfer. It had a crew of two, and it weighed 7.3 tons.

1939 H kl 6k; Sd.Kfz.11/3 Mittlerer Sprühkraftwagen. This was a medium bulk-contamination vehicle, weighing 7.5 tons, and fitted with an automatic spraying apparatus and storage tank. It had a crew of two (see page 91).

1939 H kl 6s; Sd.Kfz.11/2 Mittlerer Entgiftungskraftwagen. This was a 6.7 ton medium decontamination vehicle, fitted with a spreader-hopper at the rear. Bulk chemicals were contained in drums on a special rack at the rear. It had a crew of two.

1940 H kl 6N; Sd.Kfz.11/4 Nebelkraftwagen. This was a smoke mortar vehicle mounting smoke generators and refills. It had a crew of two and weighed 7 tons.

1940 Sd.Kfz.11/5 Schwerer Nebelkraftwagen als Gasspührkraftwagen. This was a heavy smoke vehicle which was utilised as a gas detector vehicle.

Production of the Sd.Kfz.11 was as follows:

1938	1939	1940	1941	1942	1943	1944
79	274	728	907	1,572	2,153	1,308

Mittlerer Zugkraftwagen 5-ton Sd.Kfz.6

The Wehrmacht received this 5-ton tractor in relatively small numbers (about 3,000 were produced). It was built from 1935 to 1943 by Büssing NAG of Berlin Oberschöneweide and also, from 1938 onwards, by Daimler-Benz, principally as a troop-carrier and a tractor.

Development of the 5-ton series was initiated during 1934 by Büssing NAG. It was required as an engineer equipment and personnel carrier (in which form it had a 15-seater body and was designated Mittlerer Zugkraftwagen 5-ton mit Pi Aufbau Sd.Kfz.6) and also as an artillery tractor for the 10.5cm le.F.H.18 howitzer or 75mm gun (designated Mittlerer Zugkraftwagen 5-ton mit A-Aufbau Sd.Kfz.6/1—the 'A' standing for Artillerie). The tractor version was sometimes also used to tow the 88mm AA gun. The later version had a distinctive ammunition compartment at the rear.

Chronological development was as follows:

1934 Büssing NAG BN 1 4; 5-ton all-purpose tractor for the Wehrmacht. Krauss-Maffei of Munich also built this model, which received the designation KM1 4. It had the A-type body and its Sd.Kfz. number was 6/1. The vehicle was powered by a Maybach NL35 6-cylinder engine developing 90bhp and had constant-mesh transmission, mechanical steering brakes, pneumatic road wheels, leaf springing on both wheels and tracks and torsion-bar springing on the idler. There were four wheels per side.

1935 Büssing NAG BN 1 5. This model, developed purely for engineer units as the Mittlerer Zugkraftwagen 5-ton mit Pi Aufbau, appeared a year after the introduction of the BN 1 4 and, apart from the special 15-seater body, it was very similar to it. It weighed 8.5 tons. There were also Pf (Pioniere Fahrzeuge) 10, 11, 12, which were trestle carriers, pontoon carriers and ramp-platform carriers respectively, for the bridging column. The vehicle was also built by Daimler-Benz as the DB 1 5. This model received the Sd.Kfz. number 6.

1936 Büssing NAG BN 1 7. This vehicle was built both as the Sd.Kfz.6 and the Sd.Kfz. 6/1. It was powered by a new 100hp Maybach 6-cylinder NL38 engine and had a new radiator grill (which was carried through in later models). It was otherwise automotively similar to the previous model; and it was built concurrently by Daimler-Benz as the DB 1 7.

1938 Büssing NAG BN 1 8. This model was built as the Sd.Kfz.6. It was fairly novel in appearance and was powered by either a Maybach NL38 TUK or NL TUKRM engine. Concurrently built by Daimler-Benz as the DB 1 8, the only other alteration was the use of torsion-bar suspension with six wheels per side in place of the original four. A total of 737 were built (465 by Büssing NAG and 272 by Daimler-Benz).

1939 Büssing NAG BN 9 and 9b. These represented the final versions of the 5-ton series to be adopted, and they differed from the previous model in having a new Maybach HL54 TUKRM 6-cylinder model engine, developing 115bhp, and the idlers rigidly mounted. Seating was provided for only 13 men (including the driver). The BN 9b model had a modified braking system. Büssing NAG and Skoda built these vehicles, supplying the army with a total of 687. Production was halted during 1943 in favour of the S.WS.

1939 Büssing NAG BN 11. Although a projected design only, it was to utilise the Maybach HL61 6-cylinder engine, developing 130hp. Otherwise, it would have been similar to the previous models.

Some 5-ton vehicles were also built by Skoda in Czechoslovakia and Saurer in Austria.

Production of the Sd.Kfz.6 was as follows:

1940	*1941*	*1942*	*1943*	*1944*
348	360	564	563	729

Mittlerer Zugkraftwagen 8-ton Sd.Kfz.7

This vehicle with an 8-ton trailer capacity resulted from a specification laid down by the Wa.Prüf.6 towards the end of 1932. It was required for towing the medium-weight guns, such as the 15cm. s.F.H. 18 and the 88mm Flak 18, and as an infantry carrier it was to carry from fifteen to eighteen men.

Development and production of this vehicle was undertaken by the firm of Krauss-Maffei in München-Allach, but at a later date other firms such as Büssing NAG, Daimler-Benz, Hansa-Lloyd (Borgward), Saurer in Vienna and Breda in Milan participated in its manufacture. Of the 12,000 built, 6,129 were produced by Krauss-Maffei. Most of the later models were made by Krauss-Maffei or Hansa-Lloyd, and several models existed—ranging from the KM m 7 to the KM m 12.

The earlier models of 1934 had a track length that was only very slightly over half the overall vehicle length. These were later improved upon by fitting more powerful engines and increasing the length of the track section to three-quarters of the overall length. The extra length was carried by additional bogie wheels (one narrow and one wide on each side). The track suspension system fitted on the 8-ton vehicles represented a partial development from this model to the torsion-bar suspension on other models of the semi-track range. Krauss-Maffei objected to a proposed changeover from leaf to torsion-bar springing on the grounds of loss of production.

Some vehicles were fitted with armour on the engines and cabs.

Chronological development was as follows:

1933 The first 8-ton Krauss-Maffei semi-track KM m 7.

1934 Krauss-Maffei KM m 8. This weighed 11 tons and was also built by Büssing NAG (as BN m 8) and by Daimler-Benz (as DB m 8), both in Berlin. Production was terminated in 1935. Krauss-Maffei built a total of

380. The vehicle carried a crew of eleven men and was powered by a 6-cylinder Maybach HL52 TU engine developing 120bhp. The gearbox was a Zahnradfabrik ZG55 and mechanical steering and hand brakes were used: the foot-brakes were Knorr pneumatic. The track section had four bogies with leaf springing in pairs, and spiral springs on the idlers. In comparison with the first model, this section was of increased length. The KM m 8 was the first of this series to enter production.

1935 A later production version of the KM m 8, a more powerful engine at 130bhp. New superstructure was carried through on later models.

1936 Krauss-Maffei KM m 9. This was the second production model. This was considerably improved, the torsion bar suspension now being on the idler. It utilised the 130hp Maybach HL57 TU engine of the later production model KM m 8. Apart from the track section, the vehicles appeared externally similar. They were produced exclusively by Krauss-Maffei, who built 257.

1936 Krauss-Maffei KM m 10. This was identical to the previous model apart from the installation of a more powerful HL62 TUK engine of 140hp. It was also built by Hansa-Lloyd as the HL m 10. Hansa-Lloyd (Goliath) built 222 and Krauss-Maffei built 111.

1937 Krauss-Maffei KM m 11. Undoubtedly the most popular and numerous in the range, this model remained in production until 1944 (during 1943, Krauss-Maffei were turning out a maximum of 100 vehicles per month) and a total of 5,026 were built by this factory alone. It was mechanically similar to the KM m 10 but had two extra bogie wheels per side (making a total of six). Early vehicles had spiral springing, but some later models had full torsion-bar suspension. Considerable numbers were also turned out as the HL m 11 by Hansa-Lloyd, as the Saurer 11 in Austria, and as the Breda 61, between 1933 and 1944, in Italy. The German models KM m 11 and HL m 11 retained springing for the idler wheel. Total production in Germany was 6,129 vehicles.

1939 Krauss-Maffei KM m 12. This was a projected design only. It was to have had a Maybach HL80 6-cylinder 160hp engine but would otherwise have been automotively similar to the KM m 11.

Some vehicles produced by Krauss-Maffei were fitted with wooden-truck-type bodies and were employed in Russia as ammunition and load carriers. Other conversions included the Mittlerer Flakmesstruppenkraftwagen Sd.Kfz.7/6—which was adapted to take the thirteen-man crew of a survey team attached to flak units—and the Feuerleitpanzer, which was a partially-armoured vehicle used for accompanying V–2 missile launching units.

Production of the Sd.Kfz.7 was as follows:

1940	*1941*	*1942*	*1943*	*1944*
996	1,320	1,392	3,251	3,298

Mittlerer Zugkraftwagen 12-ton Sd.Kfz.8

Development of this vehicle by Daimler-Benz began during 1931. The first vehicle in this series, the DB ZD5, appeared during that year and was intended for use by the Russian Army——probably being despatched to the secret testing station at Kazan for trials. It was, in fact, the first vehicle in this generation of German semi-tracks and its development was based on the experience gained by Daimler-Benz with their Marienwagen during the First World War. The ZD5 had the front and rear suspension units interconnected.

The first such vehicle developed specifically for use by the German Army was the 12-ton DB s 7, which appeared during 1934. It was intended as a prime-mover for heavy artillery (15cm guns, 21cm mortars or 105mm Flak). The final and probably most numerous model appeared during 1939—the DB 10.

Apart from being produced at the Daimler-Benz factory in Marienfelde, the vehicle was also turned out by Krauss-Maffei, Krupp (at Mühlhausen) and Skoda in Czechoslovakia. The Krupp version was called the Krupp 10 and that by Skoda the S 10. Krauss-Maffei built a total of 315. All of these vehicles were standardised as the Sd.Kfz.8. Not a great number were produced —in all, about 4,000. Some were used by medium bridging companies as standard equipment. During the occupation of France, the Unic concern manufactured gearboxes for these vehicles. The 12-ton tractor could be used as a troop-carrier for up to twenty-five men.
Chronological development was as follows:
1931 DB ZD5 was the first prototype 12-ton semi-track, originally intended for Russia. Tested during 1932, it had a rear drive sprocket, weighed 9,300kg, and it was powered by a 12-cylinder Maybach DSO8 petrol engine developing 150bhp. It was intended to use the DB8 MO7 engine in production vehicles, but no production followed.
1934 DB s 7 was the first production Daimler-Benz 12-ton semi-track for the German Army, and it remained in production until 1936. It was powered by a Maybach DSO8 12-cylinder engine developing 200hp. The vehicle had leaf-spring suspension with eight wheels per side, constant-mesh gearbox, mechanical steering brakes and pneumatic road brakes. It was not fitted with a winch.
1938 Daimler-Benz DB s 8 was a more up-to-date version of the DB s 7. It had the original engine and leaf-springing on the bogies (now with six wheels per side). However, the idler had torsion-bar suspension, and the vehicle was fitted with a winch.
1938 Daimler-Benz DB 9 was powered by a new 185hp Maybach 12-cylinder HL85 TUKRM engine and fitted with ATE hydraulic steering brakes. Otherwise, it was automotively similar to the DB s 8. It was also built by Krupp (as the m.10) and by Skoda (as the s.10).
1939 Daimler-Benz DB 10 was similar to the DB 9 but had a rigidly-mounted idler and modified braking system. It remained in production until 1944.
1939 Daimler-Benz DB 11 was a project only. It was to have been powered by a 200hp Maybach HL95 engine but would otherwise have been automotively similar to the DB 10.
Production of the Sd.Kfz.8 was as follows:

1940	*1941*	*1942*	*1943*	*1944*
516	828	840	507	602

Schwerer Zugkraftwagen 18-ton Sd.Kfz.9

This series, developed and produced by Famo (Fahrzeug und Motorenbau GmbH) of Breslau, was the largest of the German semi-tracks to enter service. Production began during 1938 and ended in 1944 after the construction of some 2,500.

The 18-ton semi-track was designed primarily as a heavy tank-recovery vehicle and as a prime mover for 24-ton trailers or 21cm howitzers. It could also be used as a troop-carrier for up to thirty men. One of its principal tractor roles was the towing of the huge 24cm K3 gun.

The most commonly encountered type was the standard recovery version (called the 'Bull'), which normally had a short canvas hood fitted over the crew compartment—although a longer hood was sometimes employed. The vehicle had an open body with pressed-metal sides, a tailboard, a wooden floor, and two rows of seats. A 40-ton winch was fitted. A tool compartment was located beneath the driver's seat and there were two others immediately behind it, accessible through doors at each side of the vehicle. The centre section was in the form of an open box, and it held pulleys, chains and spare cables. The remainder of the body provided stowage space. It was designated Panzerbergegerät 18t.

There was also a bridging vehicle, capable of carrying fifteen men, which towed an equipment trailer; and there were two recovery versions fitted with cranes. The first crane version was the Sd.Kfz.9/1, which had a flat deck with a 6-ton crane that could rotate through 180°. The crane was manufactured by Bilstein of Altenvörde. The crew had folding seats behind the driver's compartment and a large toolbox was attached at the rear. An order for conversion of these vehicles was issued during April 1940.

The second version, with a 10-ton electric crane, was designated Sd.Kfz.9/2. This vehicle weighed 27 tons and was intended for lifting tanks. In the travelling position, the telescopic sections of the jib were stowed and protected by canvas covers against damage. A counterweight was provided to compensate for heavy loads, and levelling jacks were normally carried in a trailer with other equipment. These were, when in use, located in special square sections. The operator was seated at the base of the jib and controlled the crane by means of hand and foot levers. About forty of these vehicles were built and mainly used on the Eastern Front.

With the occupation of France, the firm of Dietrich-Lorraine, at Luneville, undertook manufacture of the 18-ton half-track. Panhard-Leassor also received orders to manufacture this vehicle and had actually received one manufactured by Borvag of Brennan from the Germans to use as a prototype. The original order was placed with Panhard in March 1942, but no complete vehicles had in fact been delivered up to VE day.
Chronological development was as follows:
1936 FM gr 1 was the first model built by Famo and it served as the pre-production model for the series. It was powered by a Maybach HL98 TUK V-12 230hp engine, had ZF constant-mesh transmission, mechanical (self-servo) steering brakes and pneumatic road brakes. The front wheels were sprung by leaf springs and the tracked section (which had six wheels per side) by torsion-bars.

1938 Famo F2 was a further prototype in the series, automotively identical to the previous model.

1939 Famo F3 was the first production model, designated Schwerer Zugkraftwagen 18t Sd.Kfz.9. It was powered by a Maybach HL108 TUKRM V-12 engine developing 250hp, and provided with a new clutch. Otherwise, it was automotively similar to the previous model. It remained in production until 1943.

1939 Famo F4 was the projected design as further proposed development of the 18-ton vehicle. It was to have had the new Maybach HL116 6-cylinder engine developing 260 hp. Otherwise it was to have been similar to the previous model.

Production of the Sd.Kfz.9 was as follows:

1940	1941	1942	1943	1944
240	240	384	643	834

1. **Left:** Daimler-Benz Marienwagen.
2. **Below:** Krauss-Maffei MS half-track; original model on trials.
3. **Right:** Krauss-Maffei MS half-track; later model with military bodywork.
4. **Below right:** Demag D11 1; first experimental model of the 1-ton semi-track (also referred to as 11 1).

Eigengew. 4290 kg.
Nutzl. 12 Pers. od.1000 kg.
Anhängelast. 6000 kg.

IY-02247

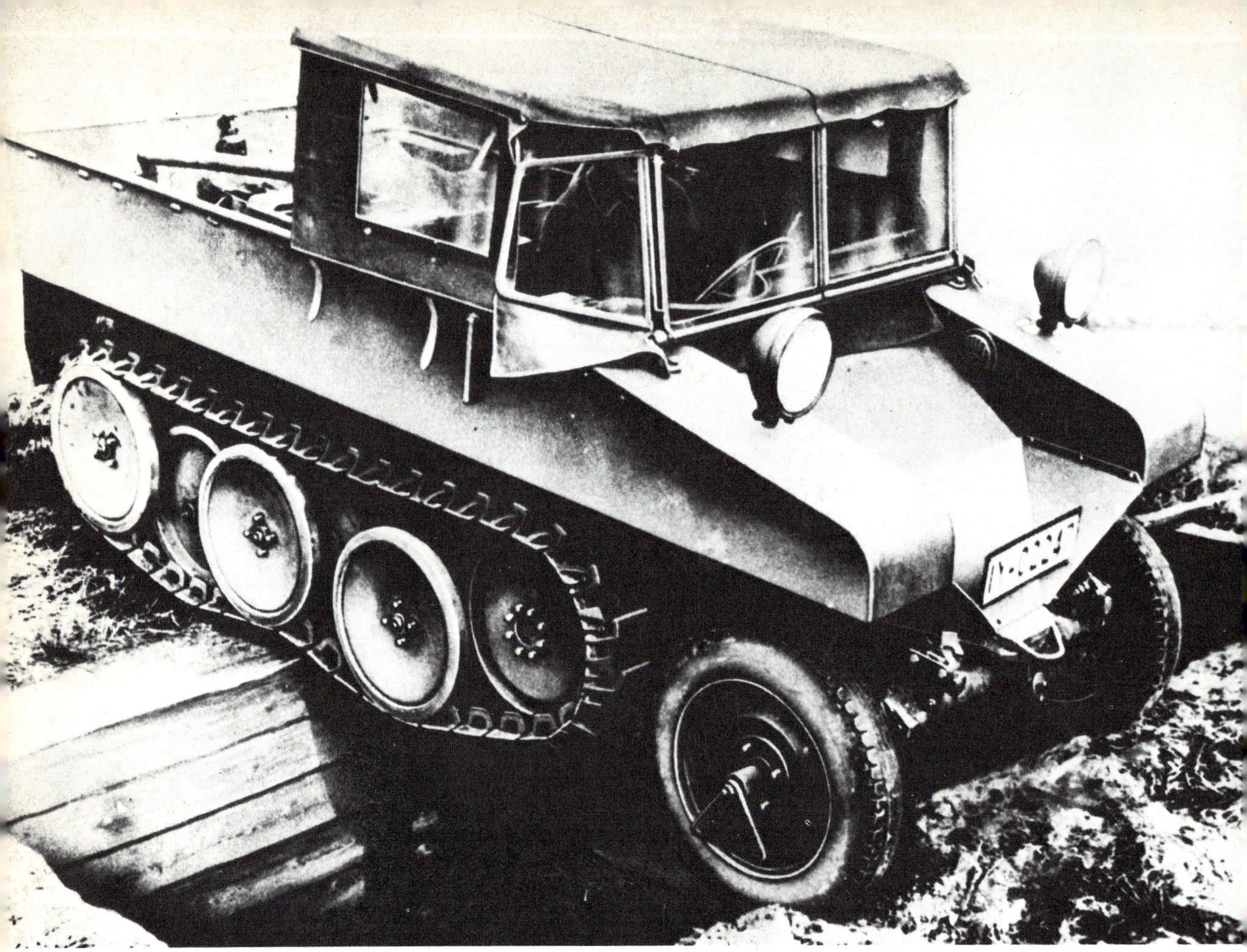

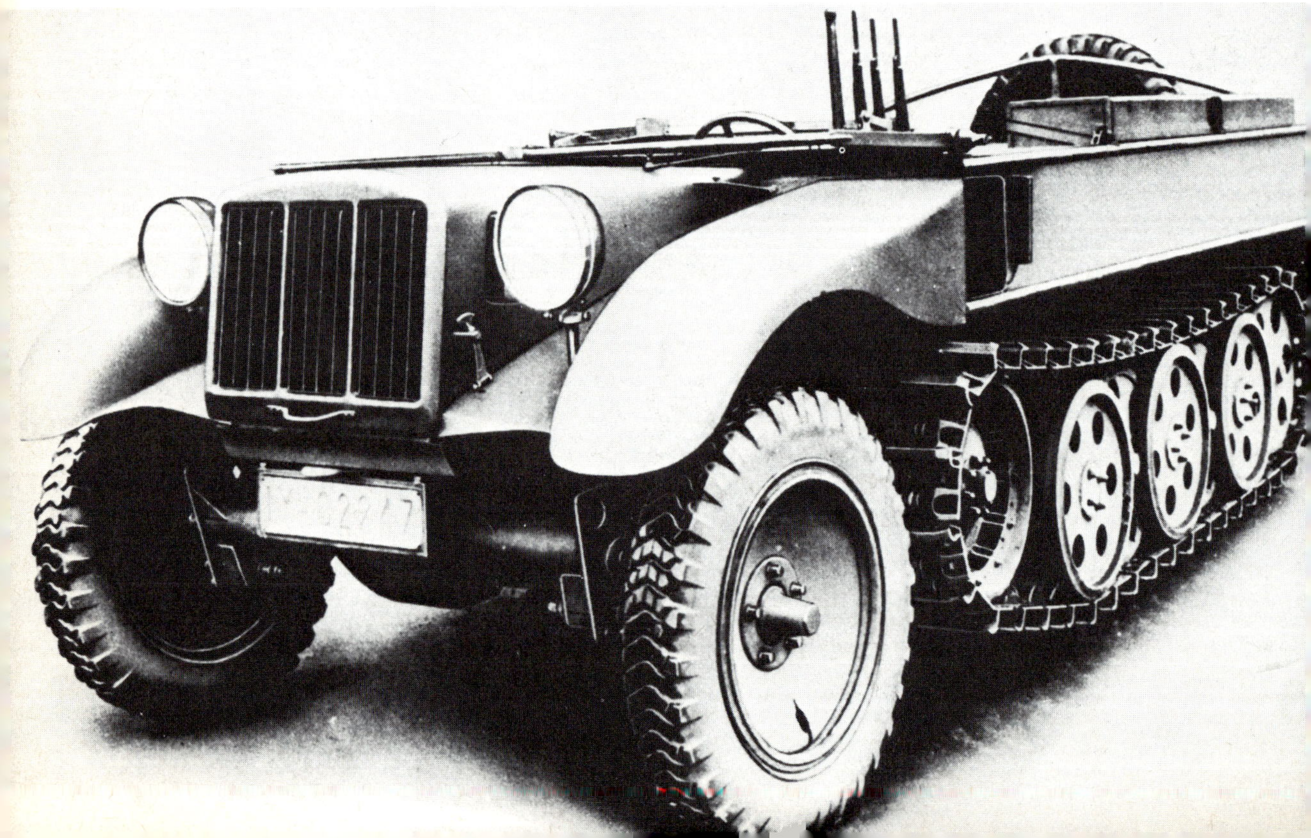

5. Left: D11 2; second experimental model of the 1-ton semi-track (also referred to as 11 2).

6. Below left: D11 3; third experimental model of the 1-ton semi-track (also referred to as 11 3). The photo shows the vehicle with military stowage (e.g. rifle racks).

7. Above right: D11 3 rigged for driving tests.

8. Centre right: Plan view of D11 3 showing internal layout.

9. Below right: Experimental chassis of the Demag D6—the penultimate stage in the development of the 1-ton semi-track.

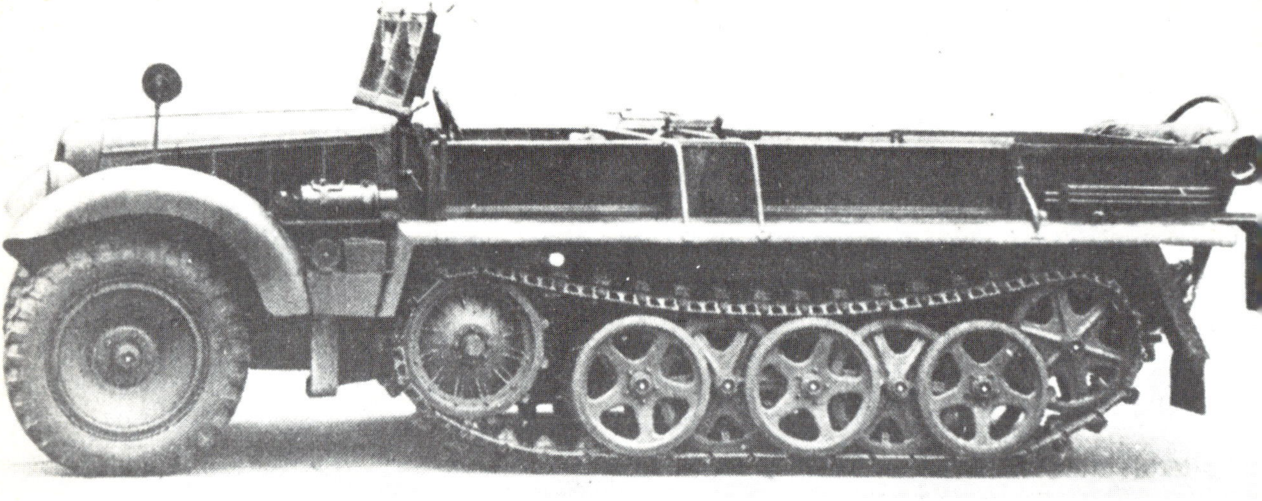

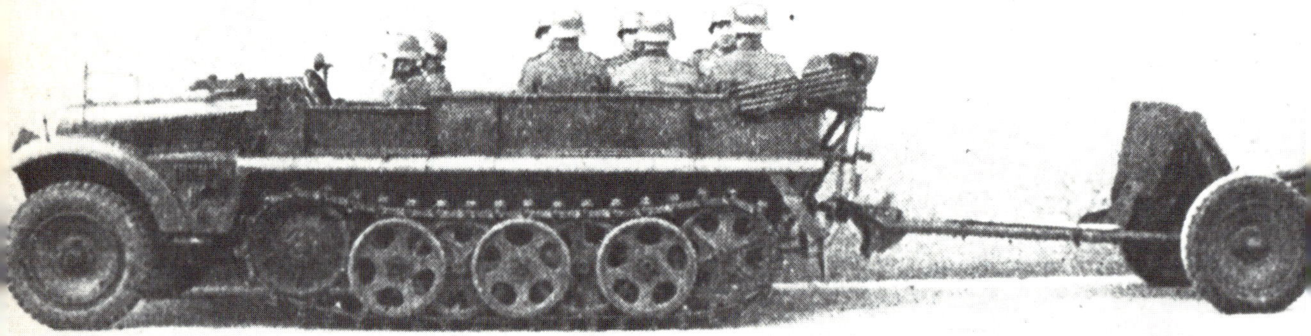

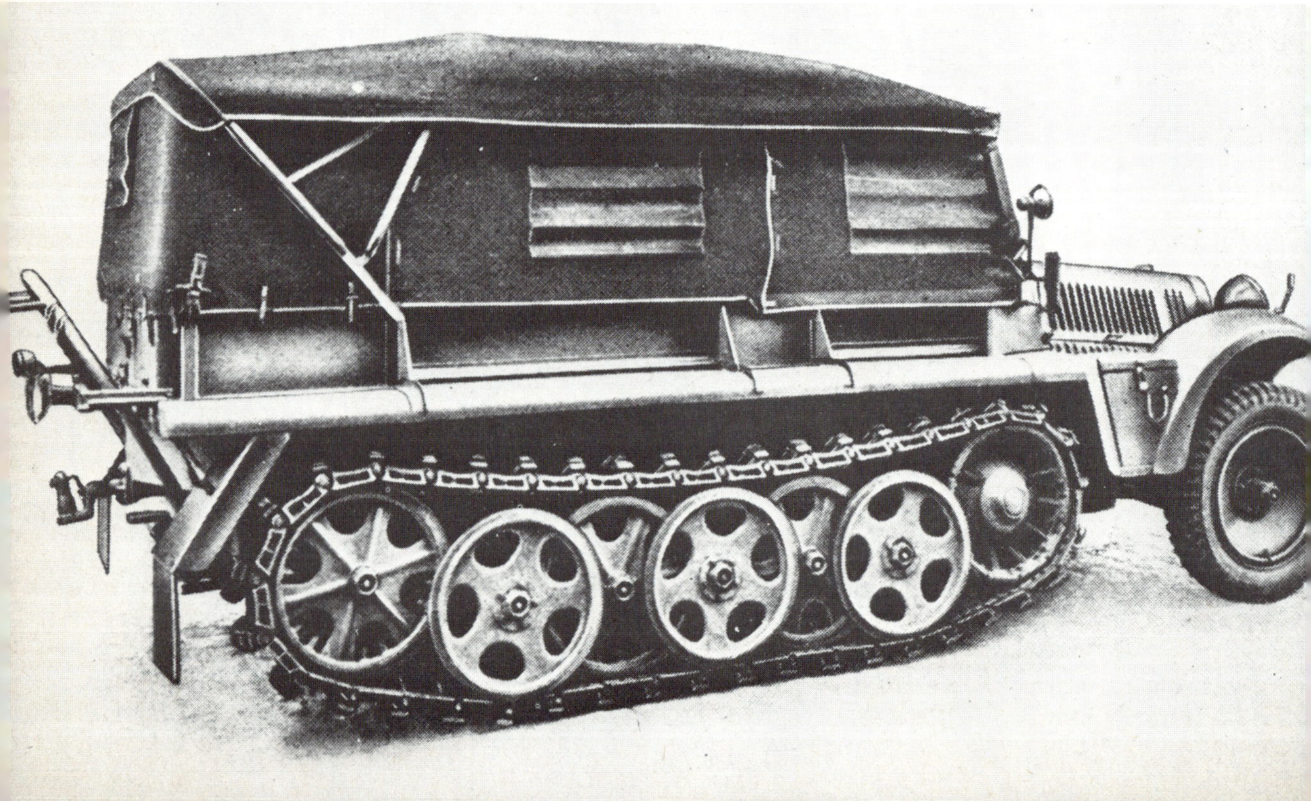

10. Left: Completed D6 semi-track with troop-carrying body.
11. Centre left: D6 as tractor for the 3.7cm Pak anti-tank gun. The vehicle can be distinguished from the later D7 by the shape of the radiator grille on the sides of the bonnet.
12. Below left: Demag D7, production model of the Sd.Kfz.10 1-ton semi-track. The vehicle shown is fitted with the standard canvas tilt.
13. Right: Sd.Kfz.10 (D7 model) as tractor for the 3.7cm Pak.
14. Below: Hull and suspension layout of the Sd.Kfz.10 (D7 model).

WH-175491

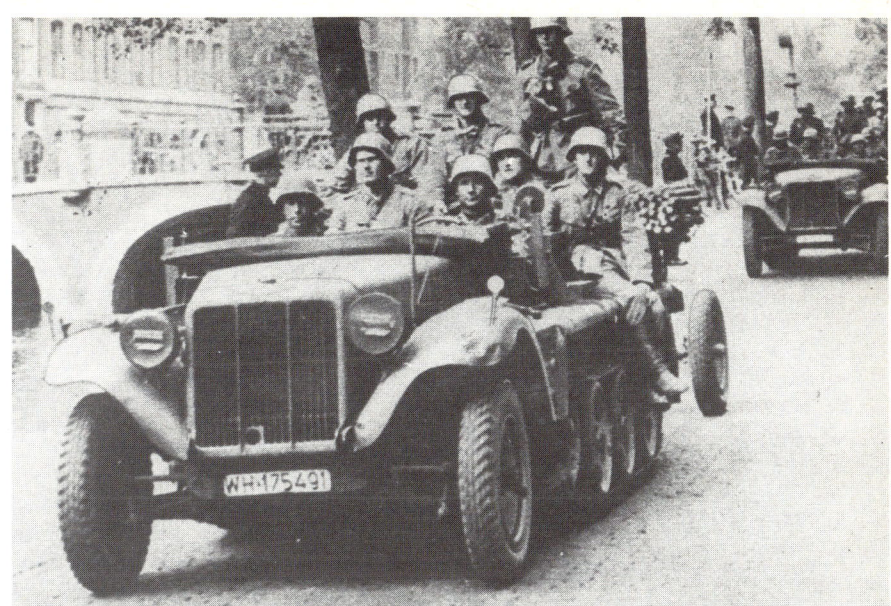

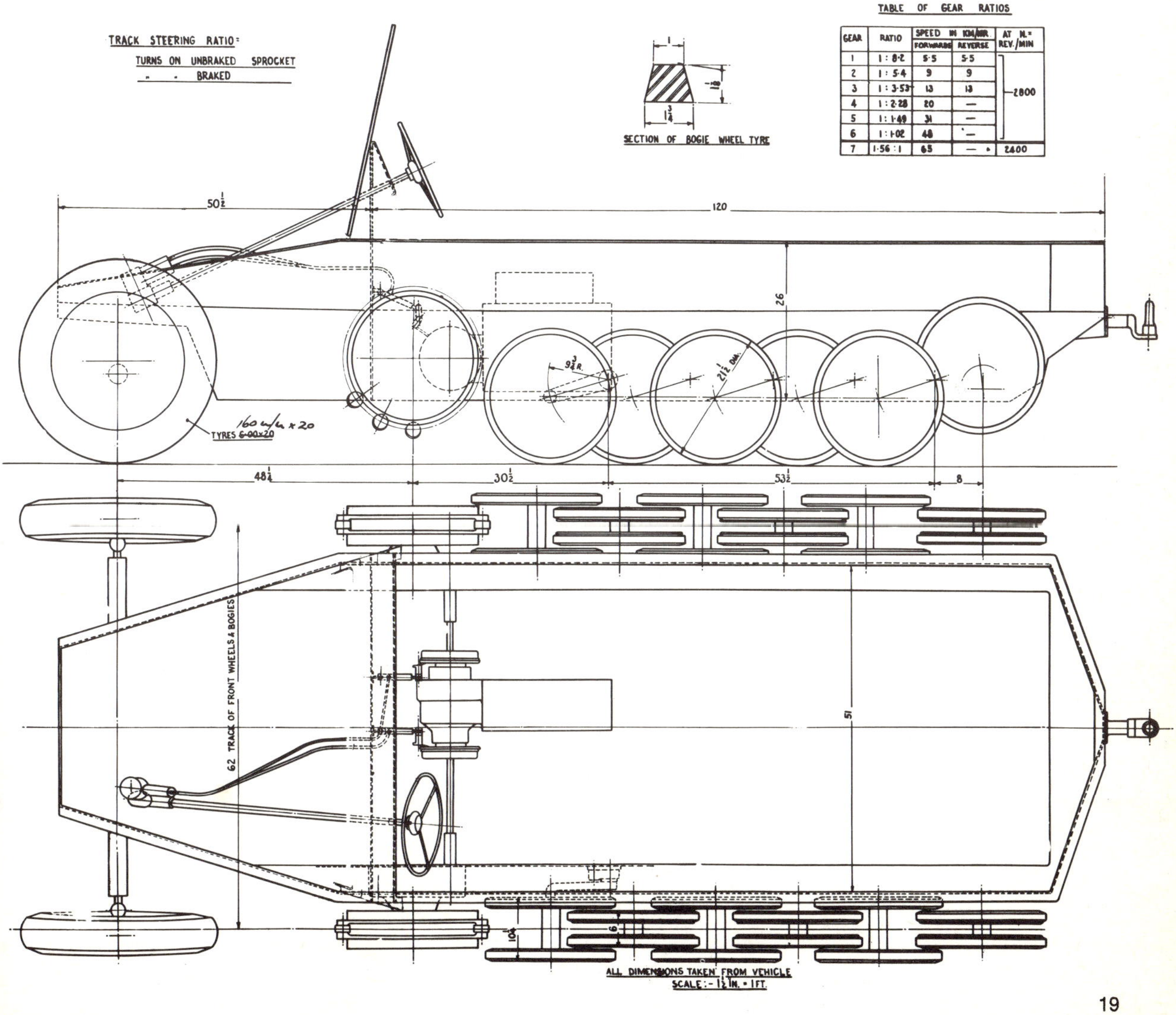
TRACK STEERING RATIO =
TURNS ON UNBRAKED SPROCKET
" " BRAKED
SECTION OF BOGIE WHEEL TYRE
TABLE OF GEAR RATIOS
50½
120
26
9¾ R.
21½ DIA.
160 w/w x 20
TYRES 6·00x20
48¼
30½
53½
8
62 TRACK OF FRONT WHEELS & BOGIES
51
10½
ALL DIMENSIONS TAKEN FROM VEHICLE
SCALE:- 1½ IN. = 1 FT.

GEAR	RATIO	SPEED IN KM/HR. FORWARDS	SPEED IN KM/HR. REVERSE	AT N. = REV./MIN
1	1 : 8·2	5·5	5·5	2800
2	1 : 5·4	9	9	
3	1 : 3·53	13	13	
4	1 : 2·28	20	—	
5	1 : 1·49	31	—	
6	1 : 1·02	48	—	
7	1·56 : 1	65	—	2400

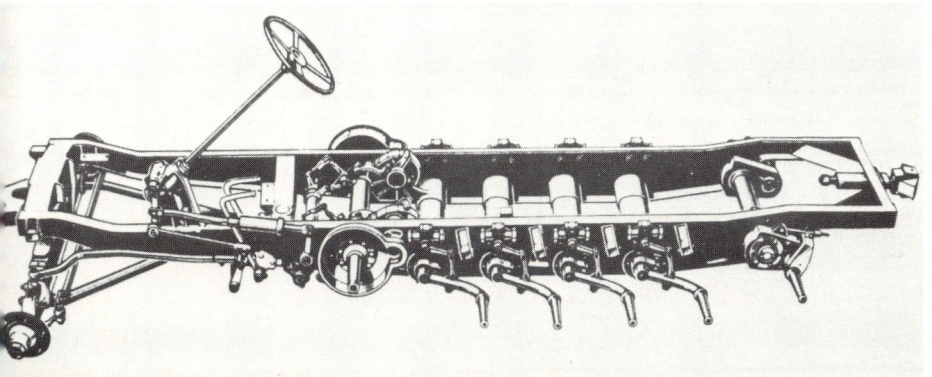

Facing page:
15. Above: Sd.Kfz.10 (D7 model) as tractor for the Nebelwerfer units of the Luftwaffe.
16. Below: Sd.Kfz.10/1 (D7 model) as Leichter Gasspürkraftwagen (light gas-detector vehicle).

This page:
17. Above: Sd.Kfz.10/2 (D6 model) as Leichter Entgiftungskraftwagen (light decontamination vehicle).
18. Centre: Sd.Kfz.10/3 (D6 model) as Leichter Sprühkraftwagen (lightbulk contamination vehicle).
19. Below: Chassis frame of light 3-ton semi-track HL kl 2.

20. Above left: Complete chassis of 3-ton HL kl 2 semi-track.
21. Below left: HL kl 2 3-ton semi-track in driving order.
22. Above: Chassis of HL kl 3(H) 3-ton semi-track. The engine was mounted at the rear to facilitate the application of an armoured body—which, however, was never fitted.
23. Centre: Chassis of HL kl 5 experimental 3-ton semi-track.
24. Below: HL kl 5 chassis being tested across country.

25, 26, 27. Left, below and above right: Three views of the HL kl 6 production model of the 3-ton semi-track, standardised as the Sd.Kfz.11.

28. Below right: Front view of HL kl 6.

29. Above left: Side view of HL kl 6 showing the tilt removed.
30. Left: Side view of HL kl 6 with tilt attached.
31. Below left: HL kl 6, Sd.Kfz.11, towing the 10.5cm light field-howitzer 18.
32. Above: Driving compartment of HL kl 6.
33. Right: Engine compartment of HL kl 6.

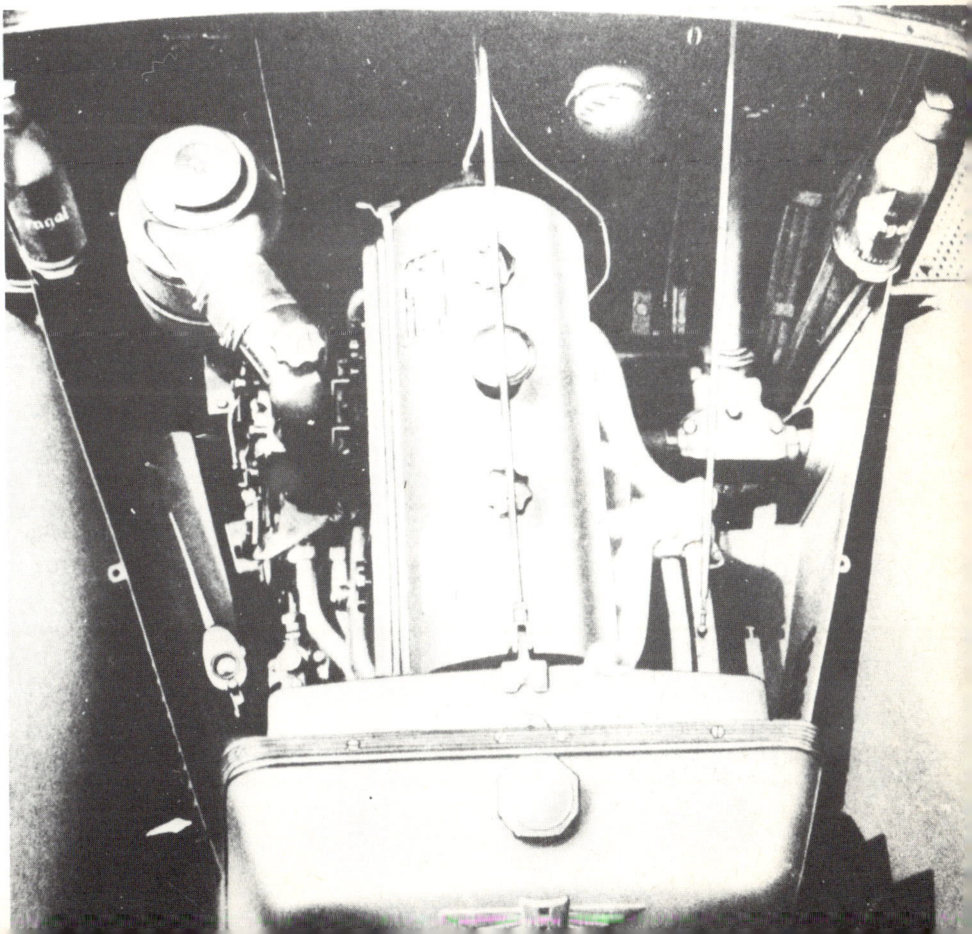

34. **Left:** Experimental Hanomag H8(H) 3-ton semi-track chassis with rear engine. It was to have had an armoured body.

35. **Centre left:** Chassis of the H7 3-ton semi-track. This was intended to have been a standardised 3-ton model but it did not enter production.

36. **Below left:** H kl 6N, Sd.Kfz.11/1 Nebelkraftwagen (smoke vehicle). The special racks for ammunition can be clearly seen.

37. **Above right:** H kl 6k, Sd.Kfz.11/3 Mittlerer Sprühkraftwagen (medium bulk contamination vehicle).

38. **Centre right:** H kl 6s, Sd.Kfz.11/2 Mittlerer Entgiftungskraftwagen (medium decontamination vehicle).

39. **Below right:** H kl 6N, Sd.Kfz.11/4 Nebelkraftwagen (smoke vehicle).

40. Left: HL kl 6 3-ton semi-track with special wooden load-platform.
41. Below: Büssing NAG BN 1 5 (Sd.Kfz.6) 5-ton semi-track with engineer body.
42. Right: Drawing showing the general layout of the BN 1 5 model.
43. Below right: Büssing NAG BN 1 7 (Sd.Kfz.6) 5-ton semi-track with engineer body.

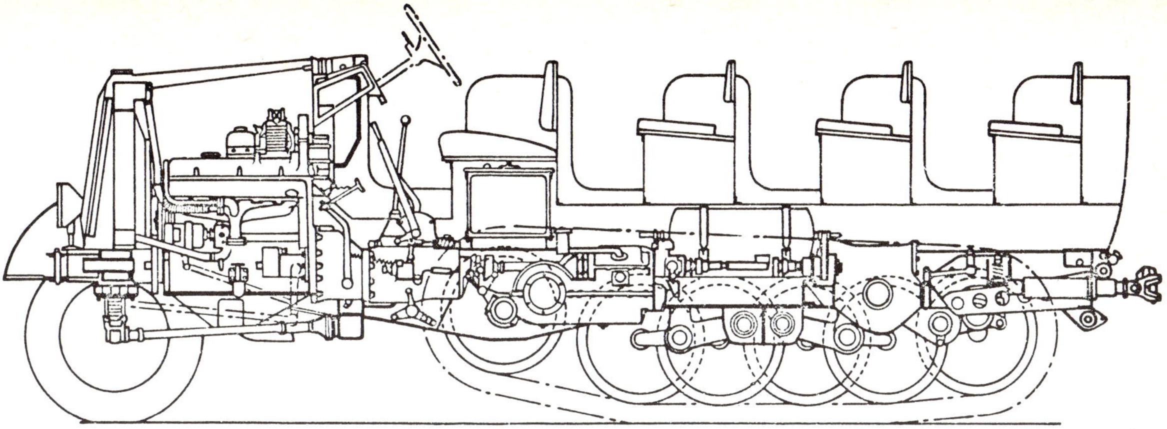

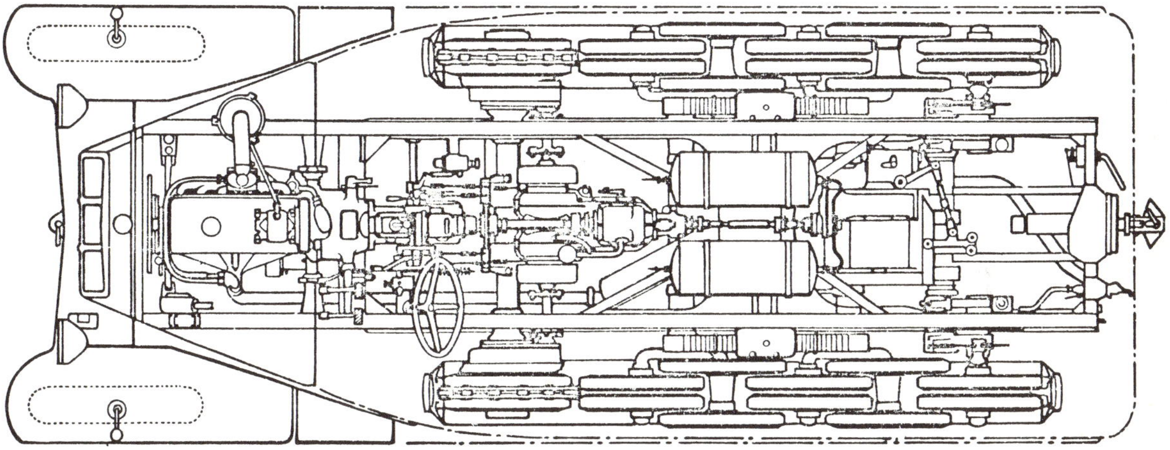

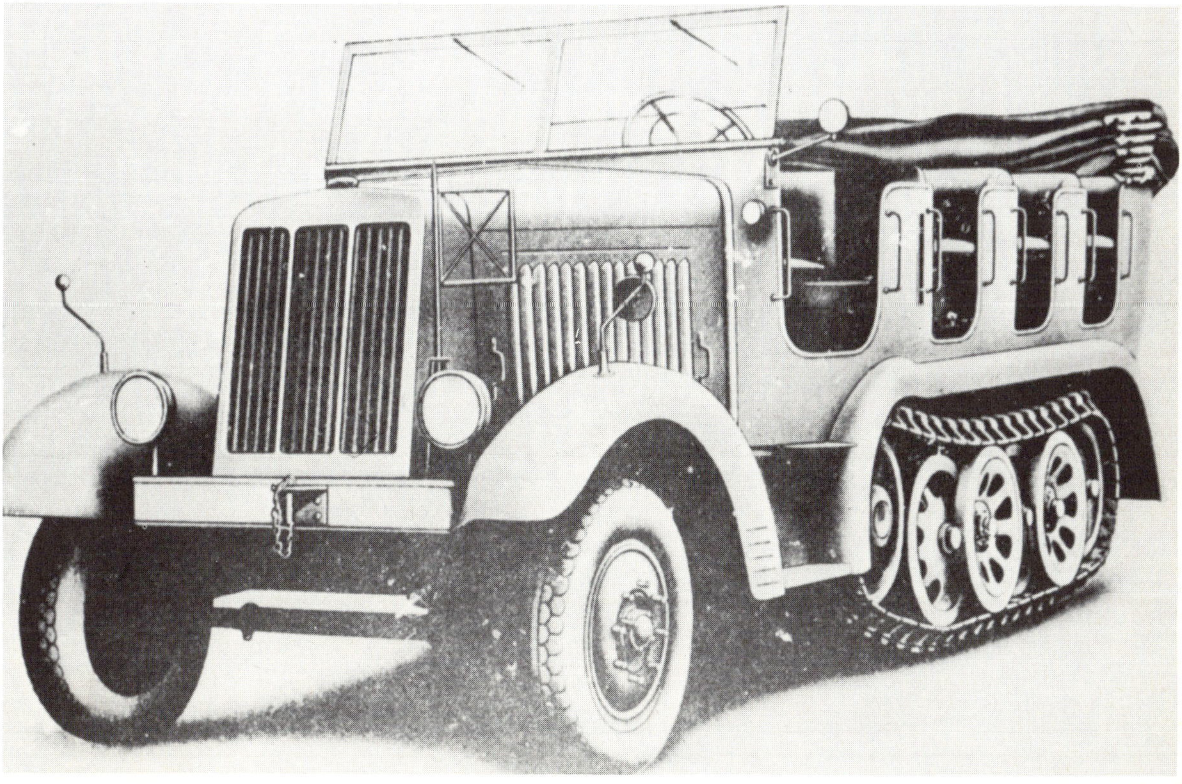

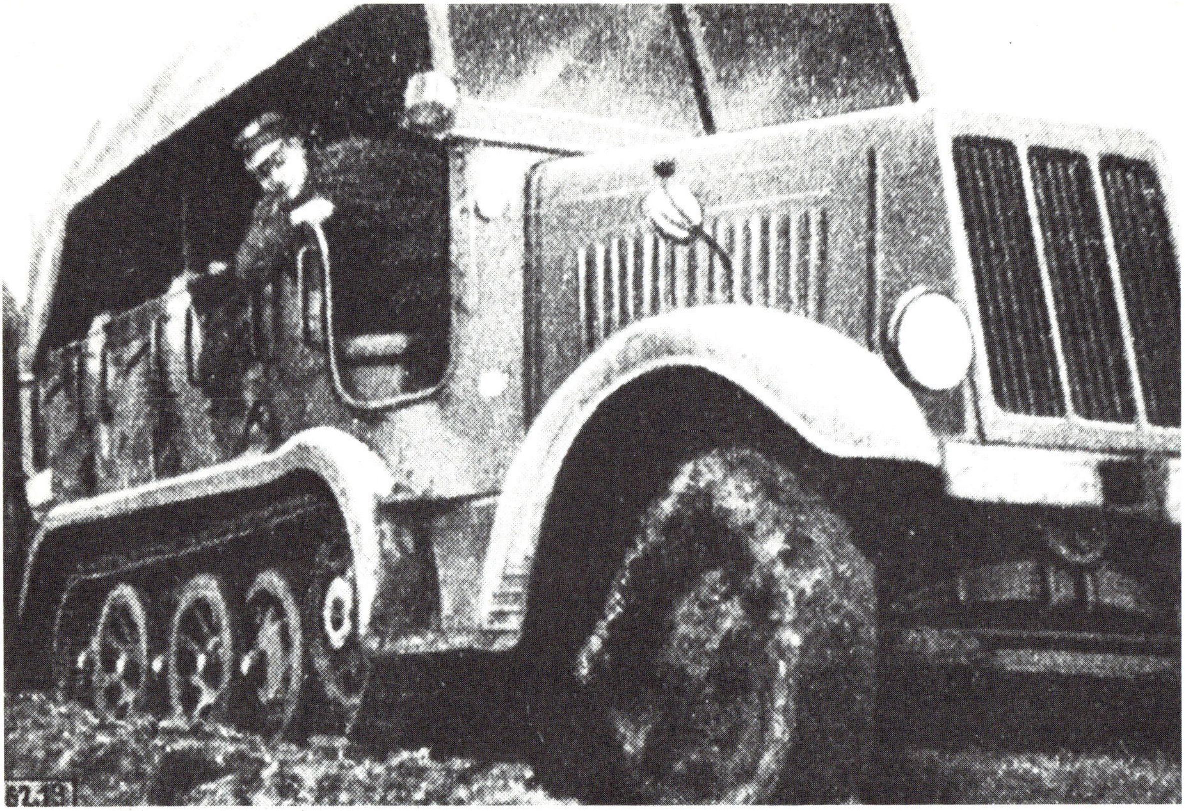

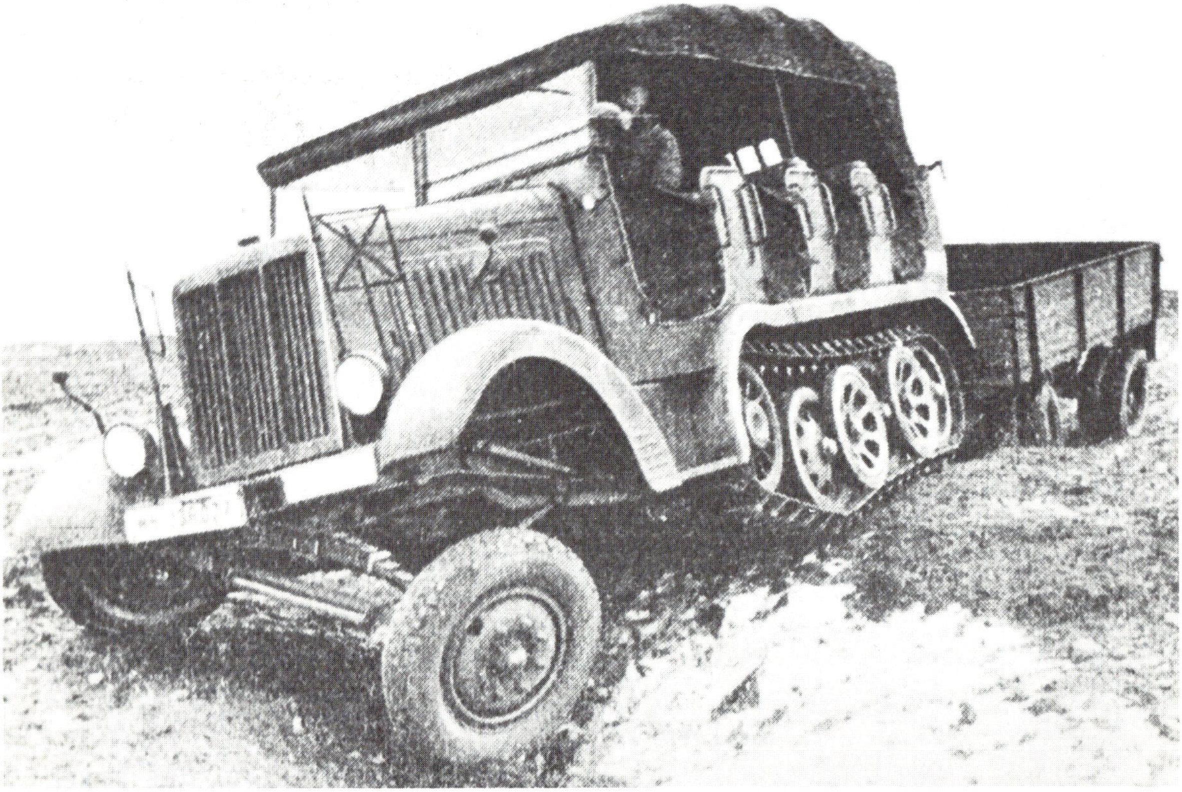

44. Above left: The BN 1 7 (Sd.Kfz.6 Pi version) negotiating heavy mud.
45. Below left: A BN 1 7 (Sd.Kfz.6 Pi version) towing its special engineer-equipment trailer.

46. Above: General layout drawings of the BN 1 7 (Sd.Kfz.6 Pi version).
47. Below: The Büssing NAG BN 1 7 (Sd.Kfz.6/1) 5-ton semi-track with artillery body. Note the reduction in seating capacity, making room for ammunition stowage.

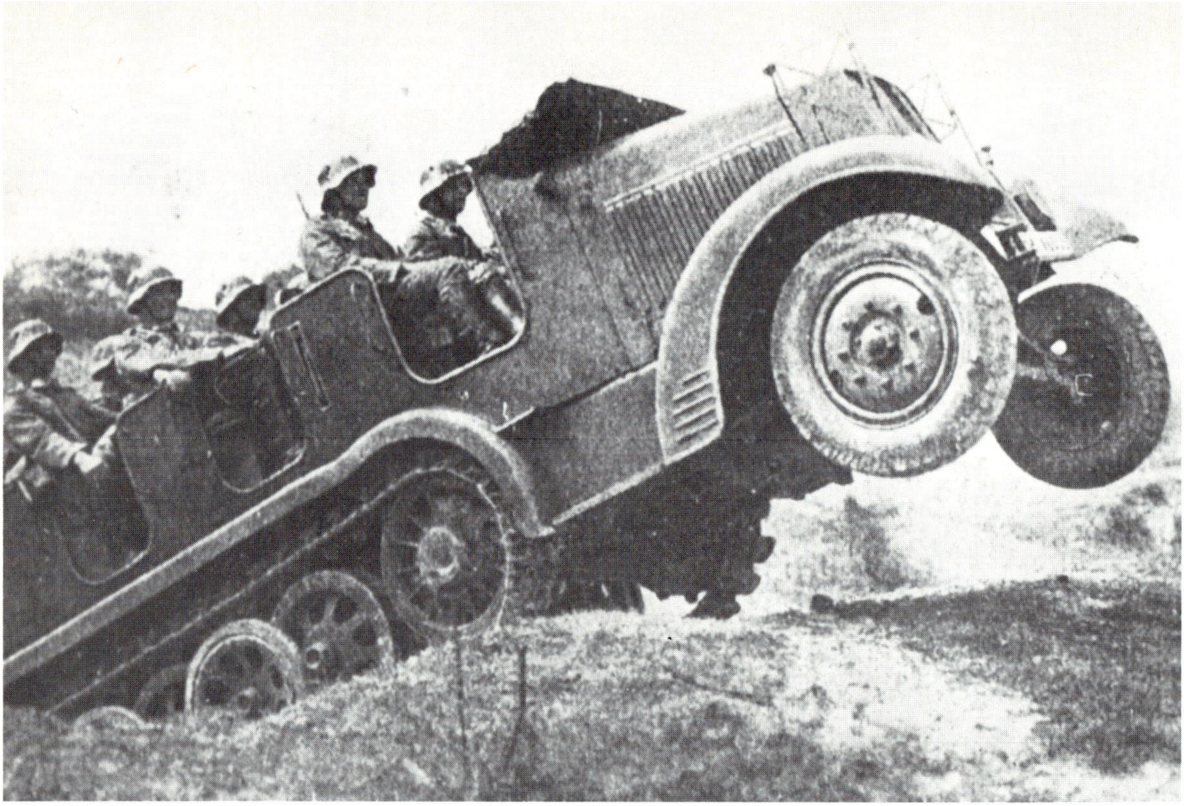

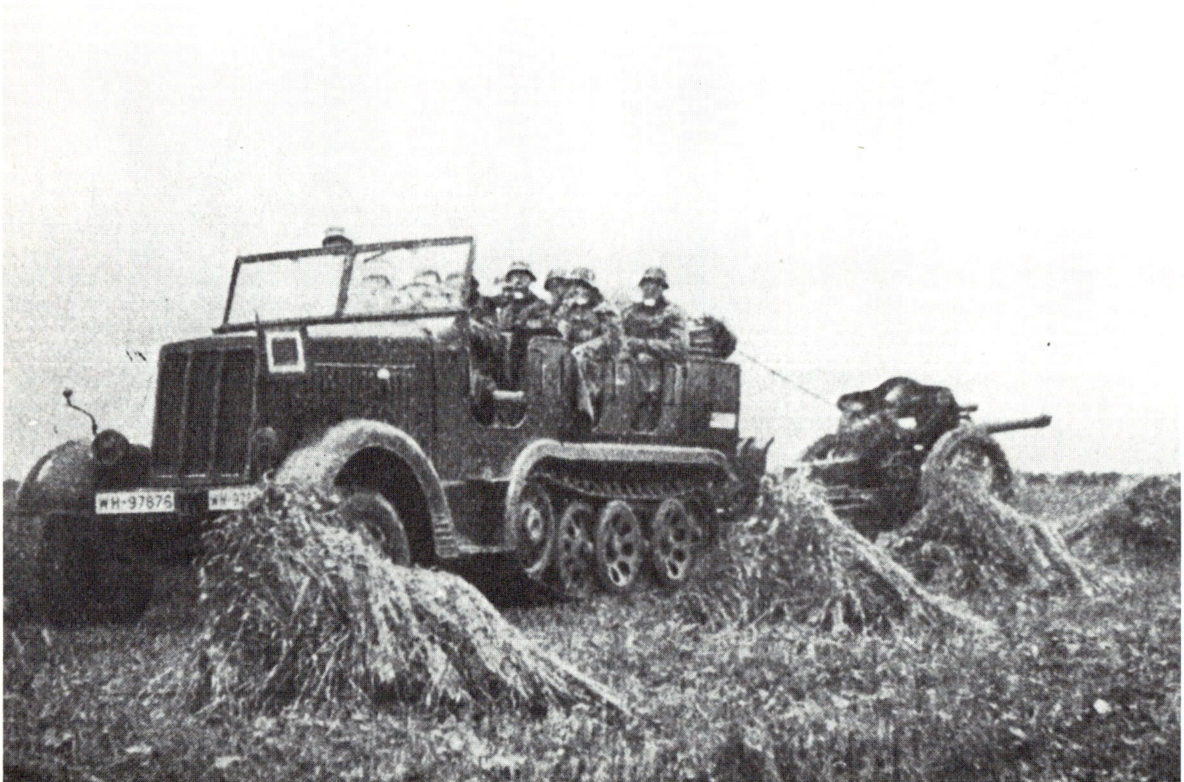
WH-97876

48. Above left: A BN 1 7 (Sd.Kfz.6/1 Typ A) negotiating an obstacle.
49. Below left: A BN 1 7 (Sd.Kfz.6/1 Typ A) towing a 10.5cm light field-howitzer 18.

50. Above: BN 1 8 (Sd.Kfz.6 Pi) with canvas tilt attached
51. Below: Büssing NAG BN 1 8 semi-track as engineer vehicle.

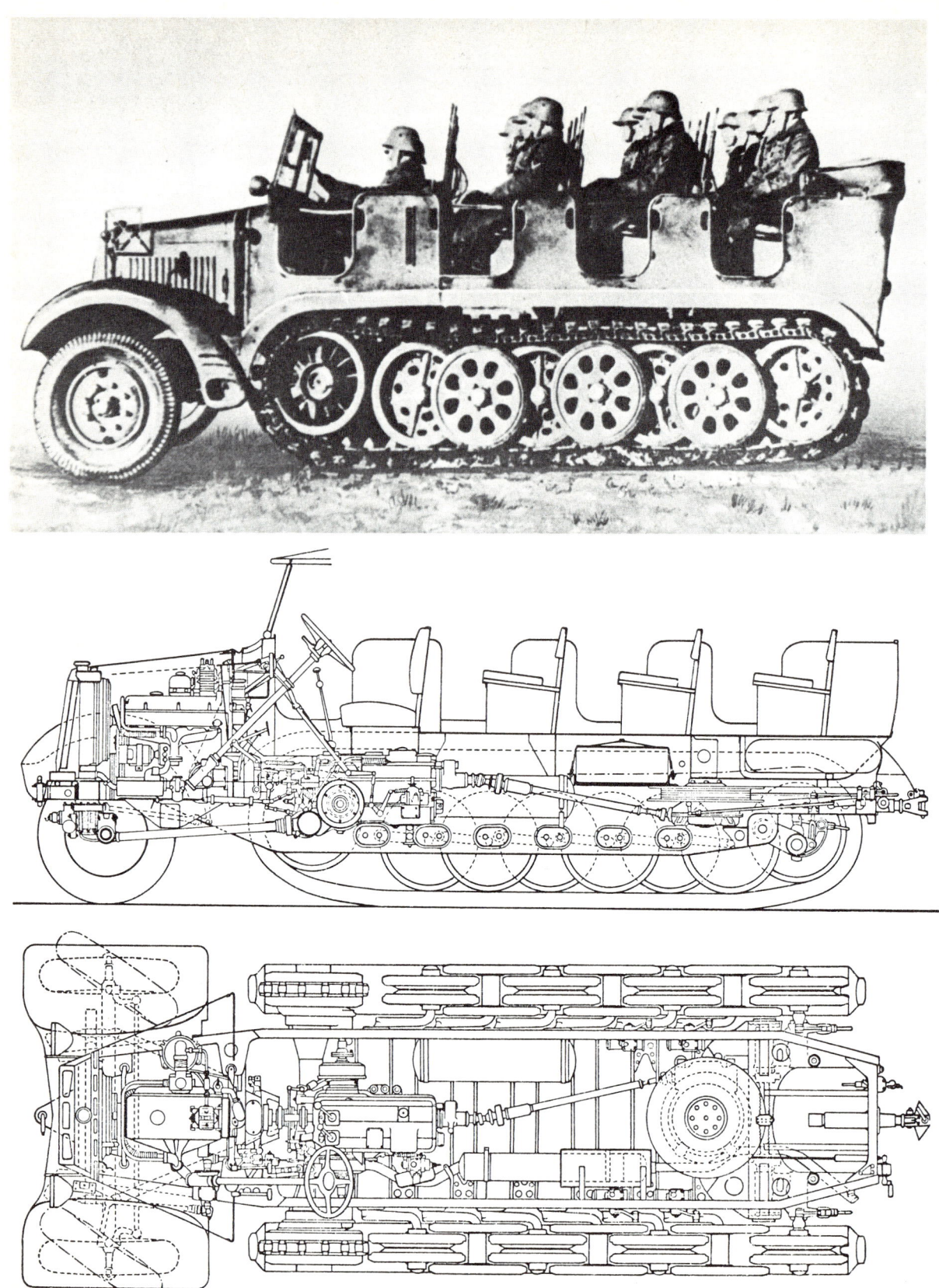

52. Left: BN 1 8 (Sd.Kfz.6 Pi) side view.

53. Below left: General layout drawings of the BN 1 8 (Sd.Kfz.6 Pi).

54. Above right: BN 9 (or 9b) 5-ton semi-track with Pi-type body (Sd.Kfz.6).

55. Centre right: BN 9 (or 9b) with Pi-type body built by Skoda in Czechoslovakia. Note the round holes in the bogie wheels compared to the original pear-shaped ones. This is the only known deviation from the bogie-wheel hole code given on page 9.

56. Below right: BN 9 (or 9b) with A-type body (Sd.Kfz.6/1).

57. Above left: BN 9 (or 9b) with A-type body towing the 10.5cm light field-howitzer 18.

58, 59. Centre and below left: Two views of the KM m 8 in use with artillery units.

60. Above: Krauss-Maffei KM m 8 8-ton semi-track.

61. Right: The automotive layout of the KM m 8 chassis.

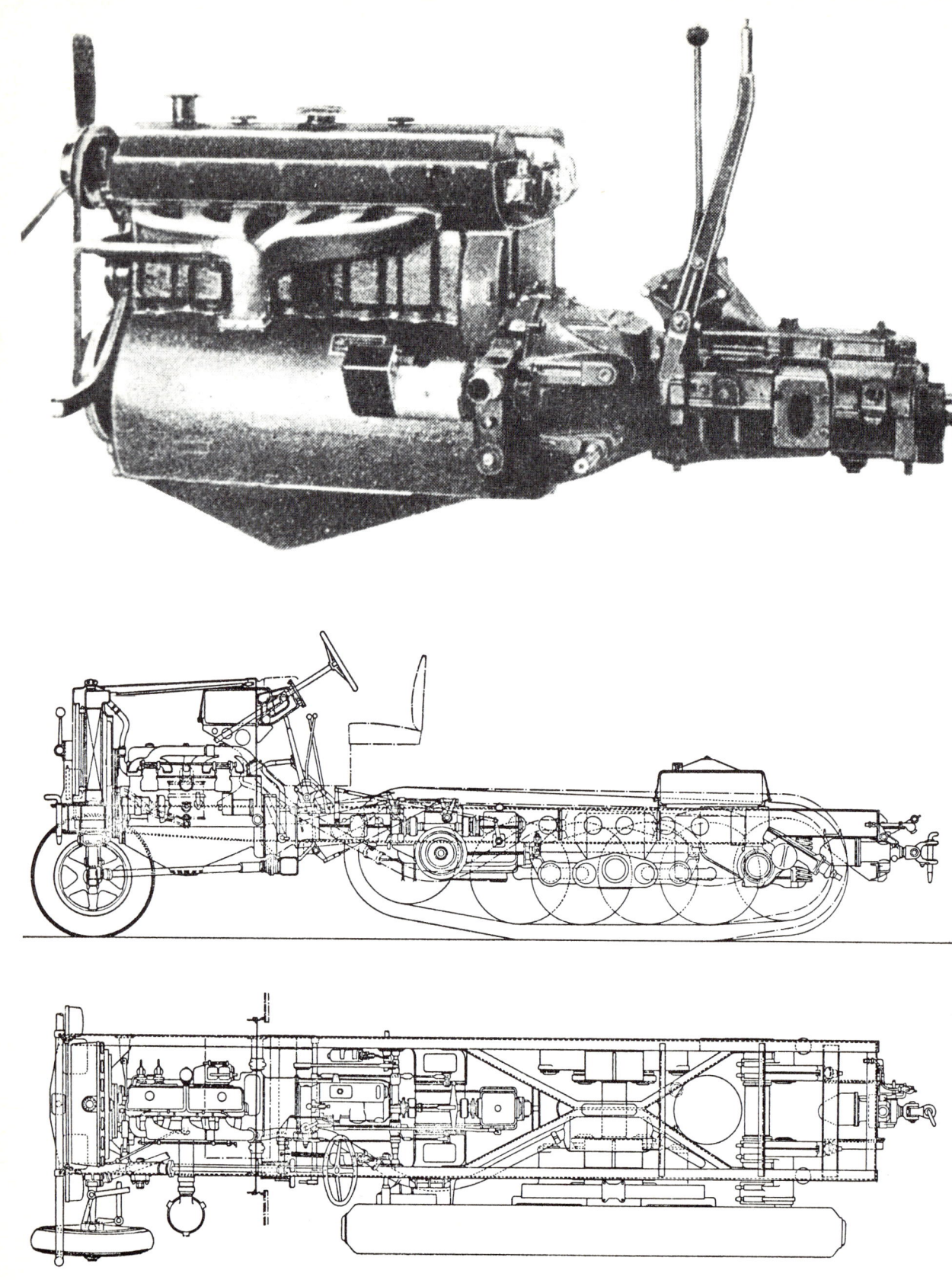

62. Left: The 6-cylinder Maybach HL 52 TU engine of the KM m 8.

63. Below left: General layout drawings of the KM m 8.

64, 65. Right and centre right: Two views of the later production model of the KM m 8 with more powerful engine. Note the track-guard.

66. Below right: The KM m 9 8-ton semi-track towing a special tank-transporter trailer for the Pz.Kpfw.II light tank.

67. Above left: The KM m 9, with a tank being winched on to the trailer.

68. Centre left: Chassis of the 8-ton semi-tracks KM m 9 and 10, which were practically identical.

69. Left: The KM m 10 model on proving trials.

70. Above right: The KM m 11 8-ton semi-track—made in greater quantities than any other of the semi-track models.

71. Right: Nearside view of the KM m 11.

72, 73 Above and left: Two three-quarter rear views of the KM m 11 chowing the vehicle with and without canvas tilt.

74. Above right: KM m 11 towing the 8.8cm Flak during acceptance trials.

75. Centre right: KM m 11 towing the 8.8cm Flak under combat conditions.

76. Right: Borgward version of the KM m 11. This vehicle has an armoured cover over the winch housing at the front of the vehicle.

48

77. Above left: Another view of the Borgward version of the KM m 11.

78. Below left: Breda 61, an Italian-produced version of the KM m 11.

79. Above: KM m 11 vehicles in production at Krauss-Maffei.

80. Below: KM m 11 as Sd.Kfz.7/6 Mittlerer Flakmesstruppenkraftwagen (medium anti-aircraft ranging vehicle).

81, 82: Left and centre left:
KM m 11 partially armoured
as Feuerleitpanzer (V-2
missile direction vehicle).
**83. Below left and above
right:** Two views of the
experimental Daimler-Benz
ZD-5 semi-track for the
12-ton class.
85. Centre right:
Daimler-Benz DB s 7
12-ton semi-track.
86. Below right: DB s 7
undergoing acceptance
trials with the Wehrmacht.

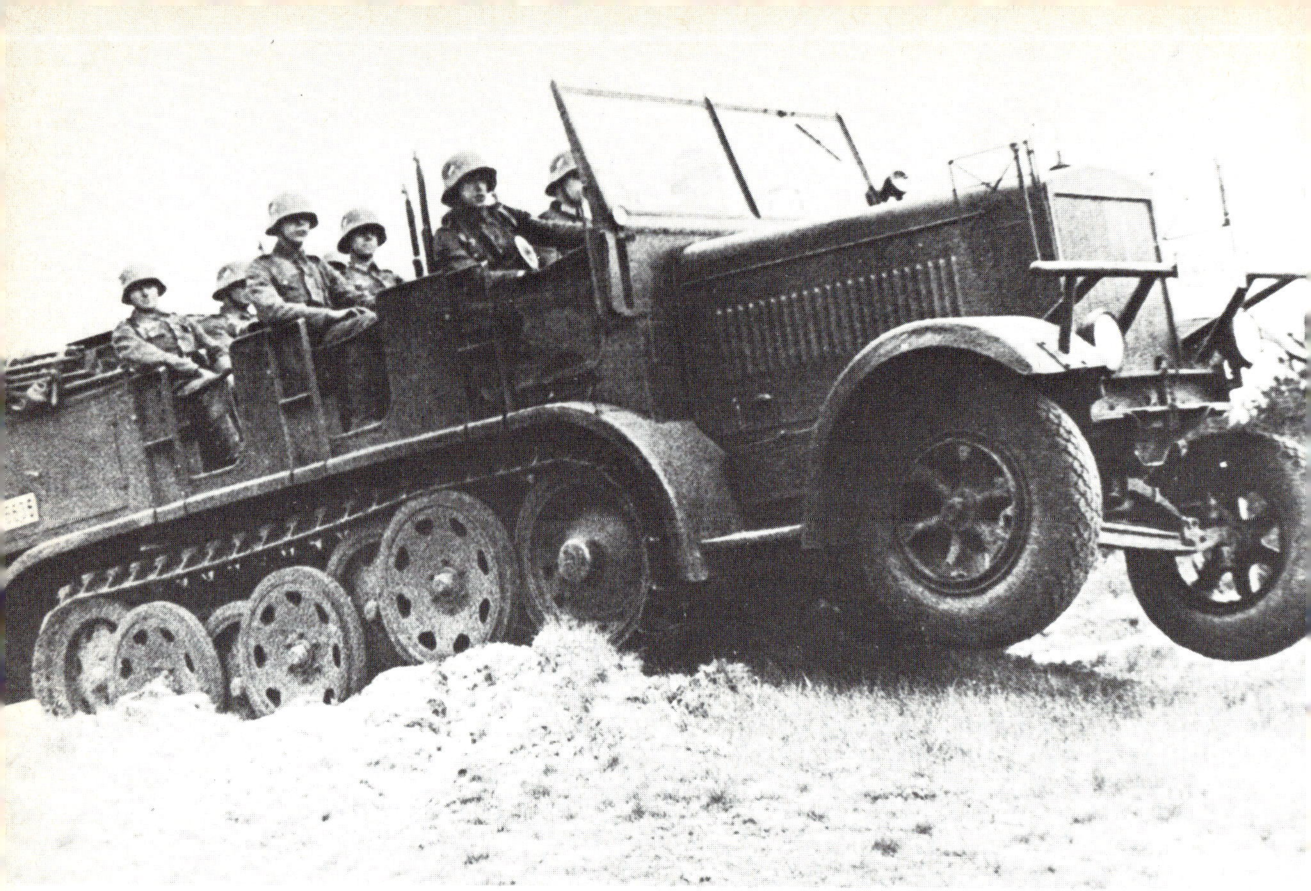

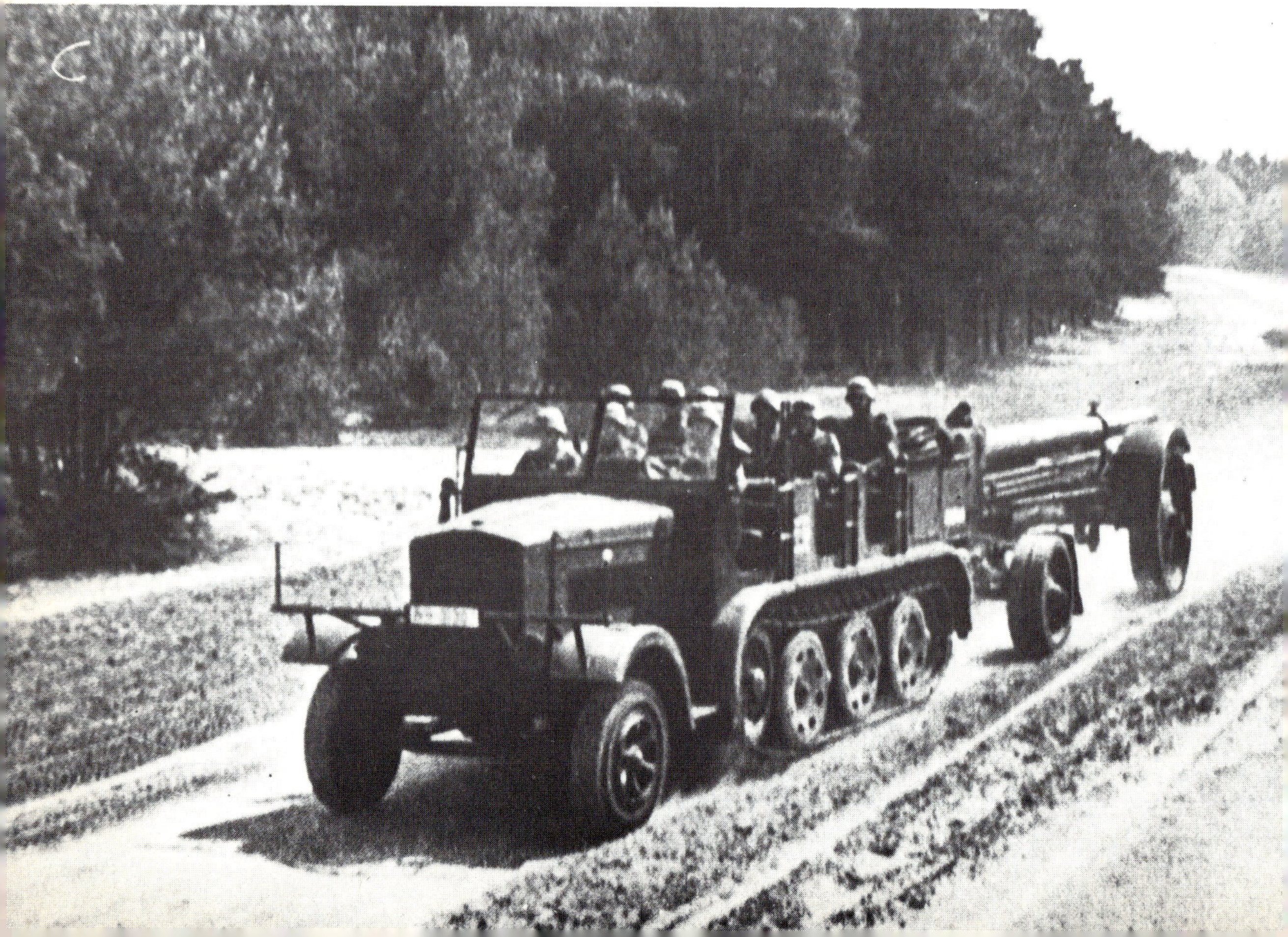

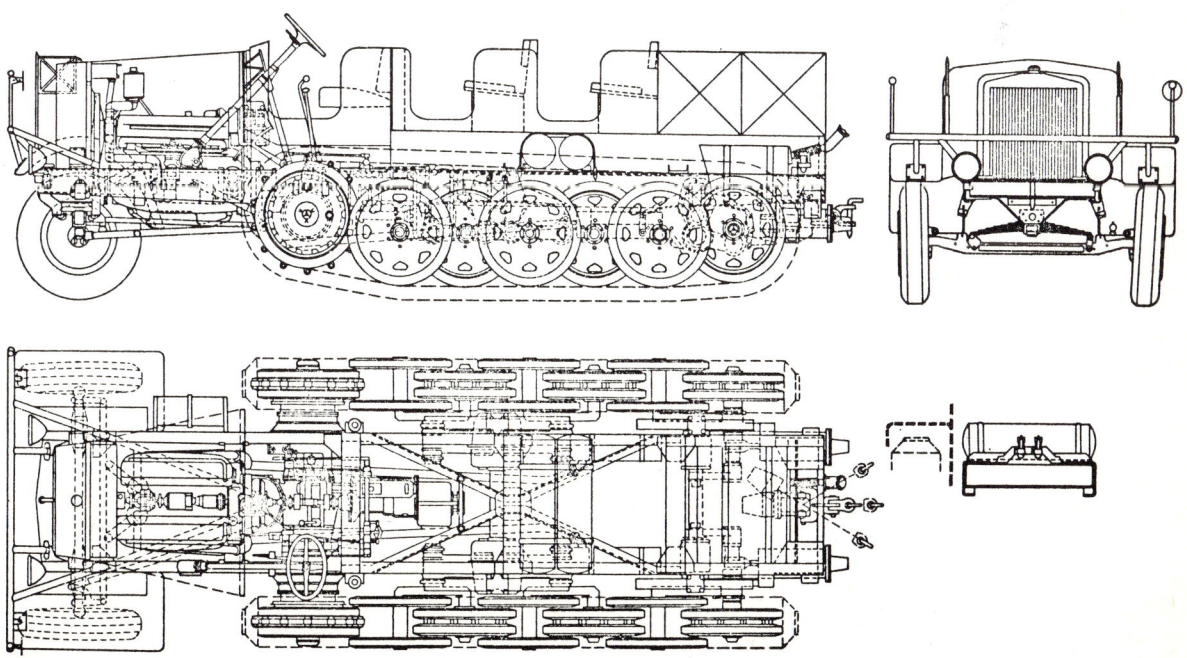

87, 88. Left: DB s 7 in service with the Wehrmacht,
taking part in exercises during the 1930s.
89. Above: DB s 7 with dozer-blade attachment,
clearing snow.
90. Below: General arrangement drawings of the DB s 7.

91. **Left:** The DB s 8—an improved version of the DB s 7 12-ton semi-track.
92. **Below left:** DB s 8 in use with Luftwaffe troops.
93. **Right:** The DB 9 12-ton semi-track model.
94. **Below right:** The DB 9 undergoing acceptance trials.

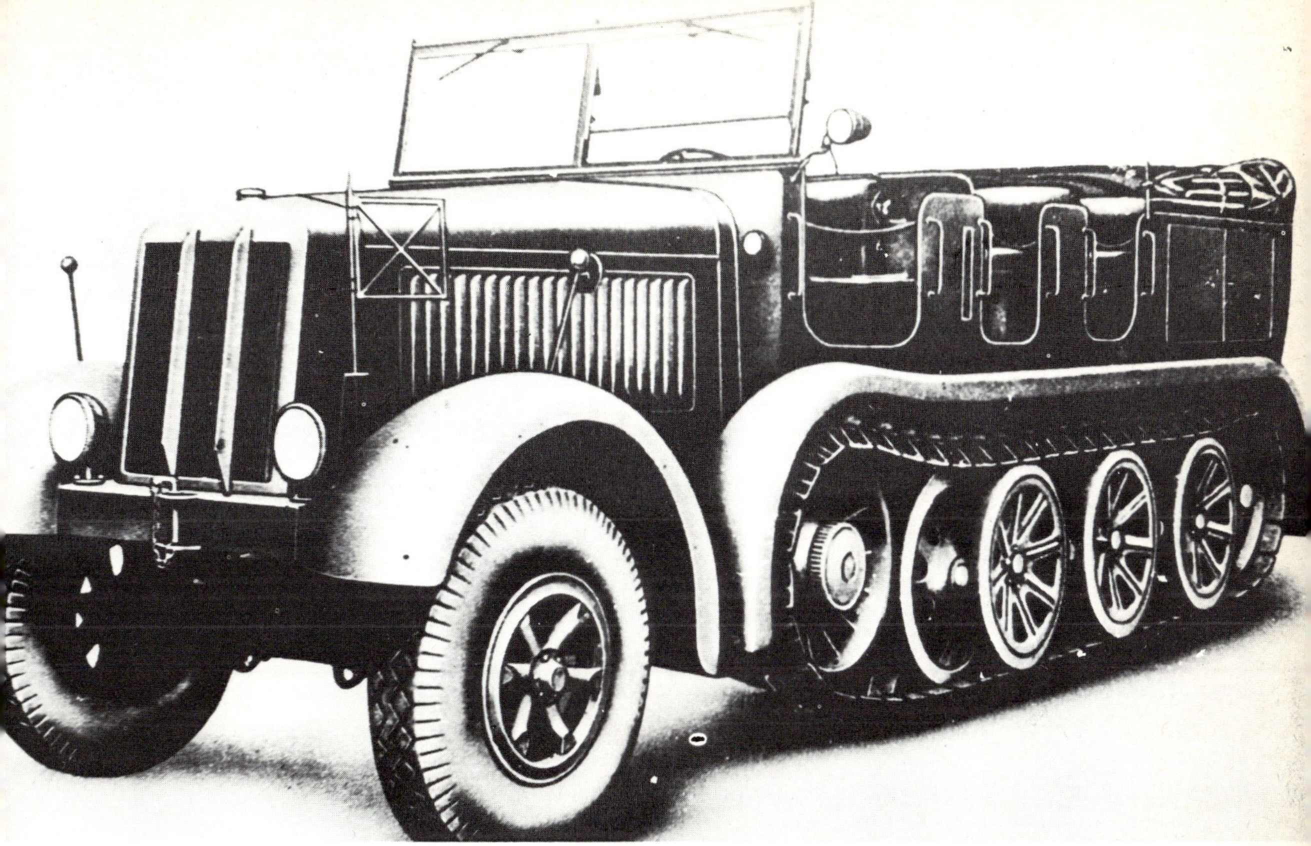

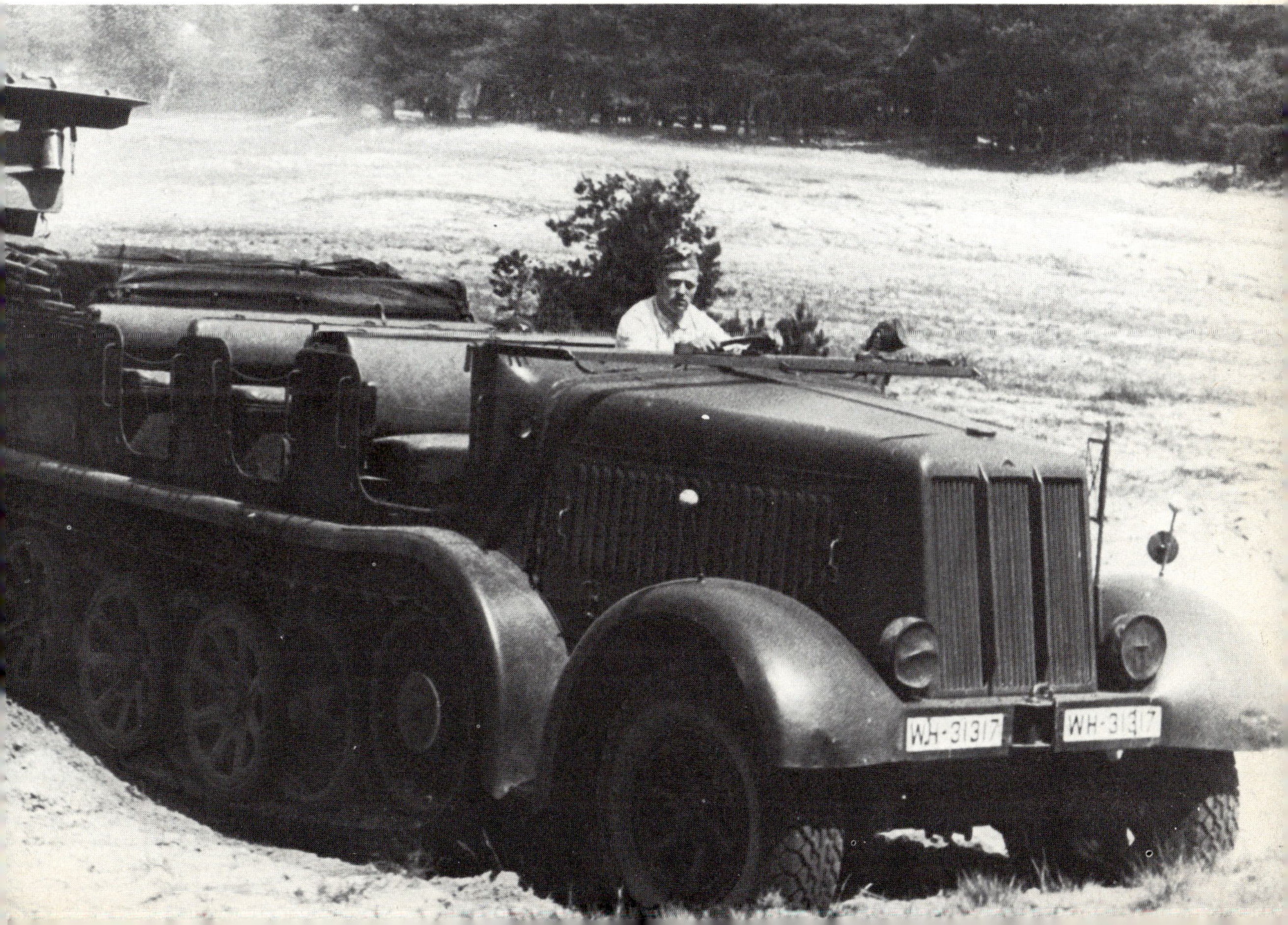
WH-31317
WH-31317

95. Left: The DB 9 in use on the Russian front.
96. Below: The DB 10—final production model of the 12-ton semi-track series. Note the solid disc hubs on the tyred wheels.
97. Above right: Nearside view of the DB 10 showing personnel seating arrangements.
98. Centre right: Offside view of the DB 10.
99. Below right: DB 10 fitted with dozer blade.

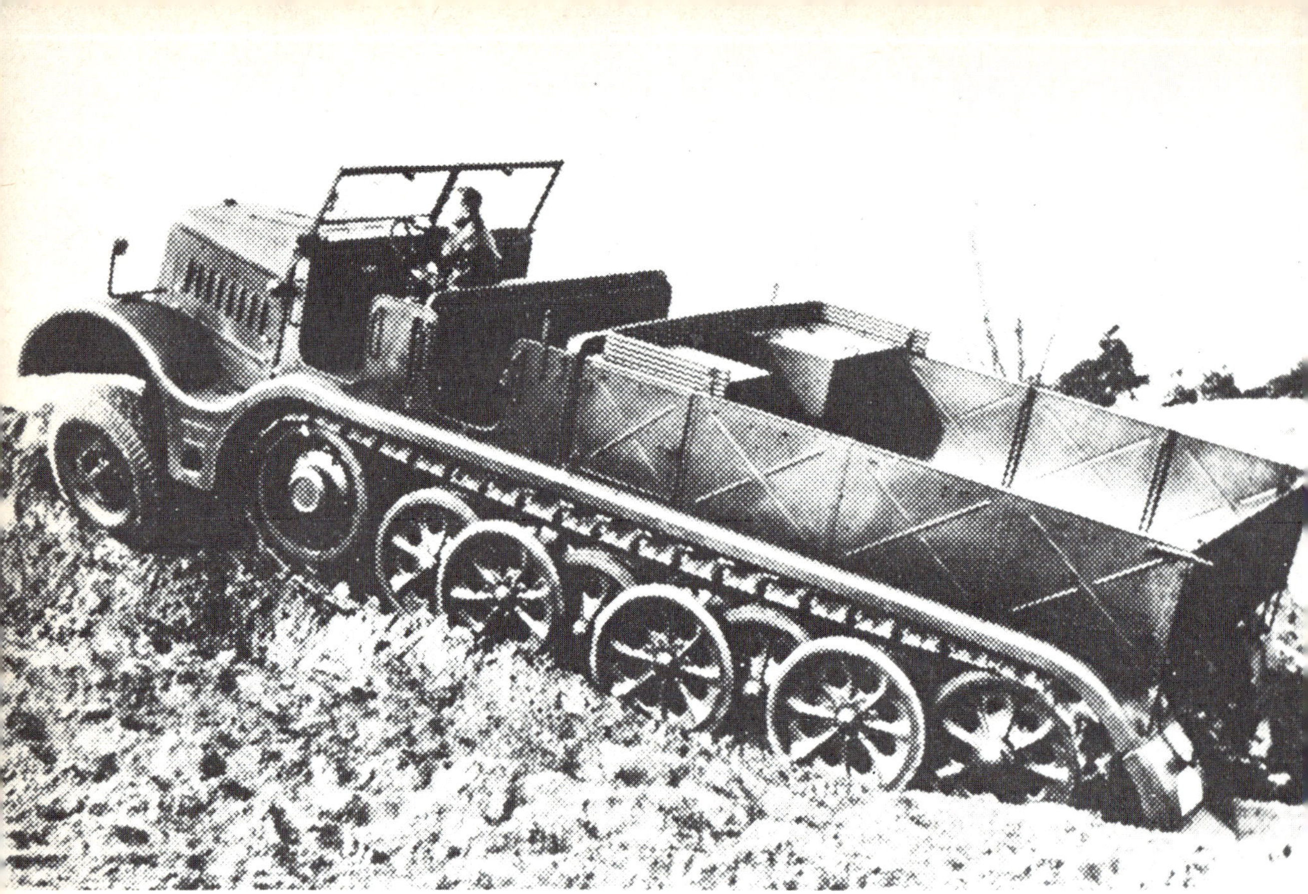

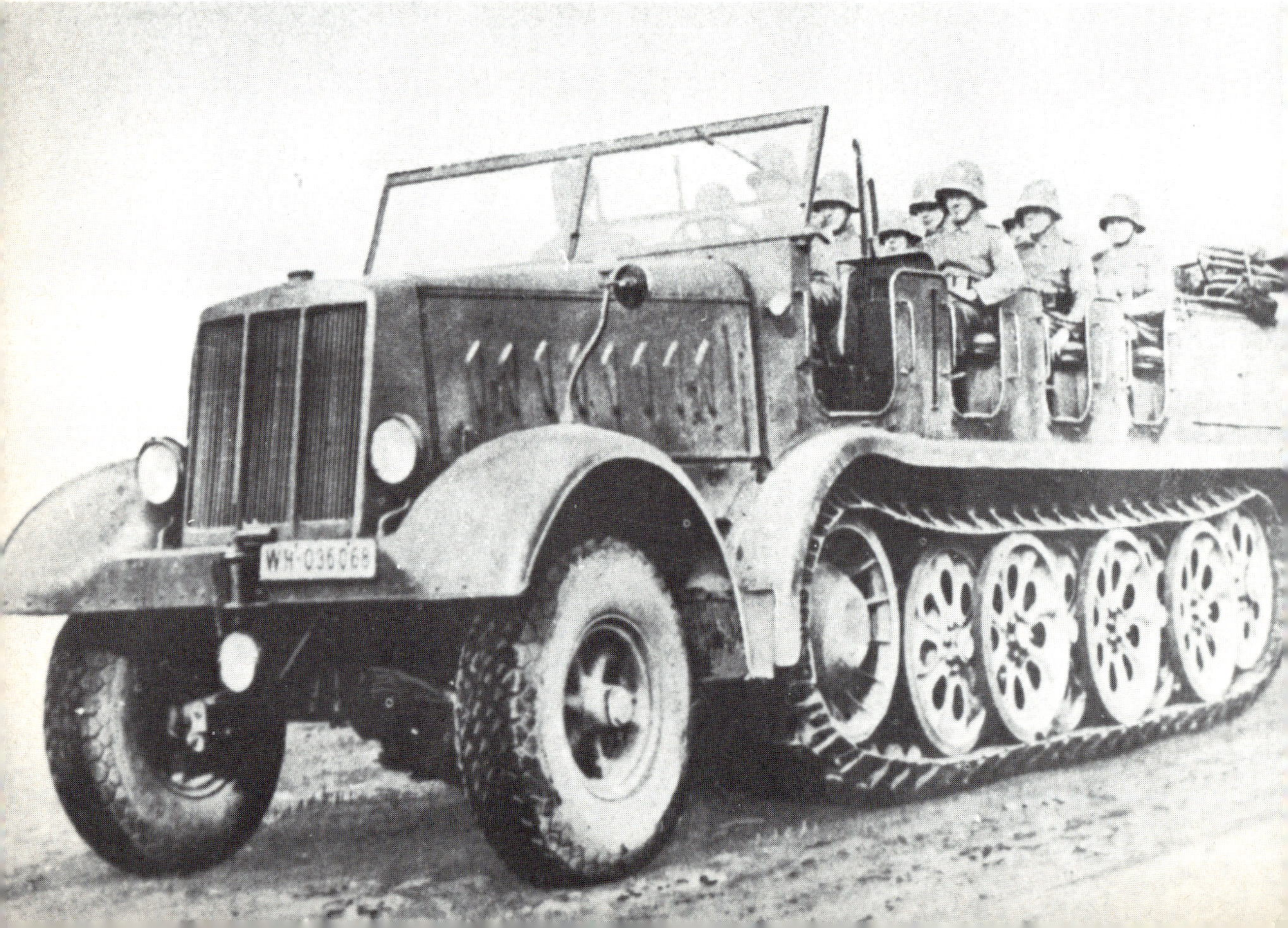

100. Left: Famo F2 prototype of the Sd.Kfz.9 18-ton semi-track.
101. Below left: Famo F3 production model of Sd. Kfz.9 shown as an artillery tractor with four rows of seats.
102, 103, 104. Right: Three views of the 18-ton Sd.Kfz.9 recovery-tractor version with two rows of seats.

105. Top: Sd.Kfz.9/1, 18-ton semi-track mounting a 6-ton crane.
106. Centre: Another view of the Sd.Kfz.9/1.
107. Below: Sd.Kfz.9/2, 18-ton semi-track mounting a 10-ton crane, in travelling order.

108. Top: Nearside view of Sd.Kfz.9/2 in travelling order.
109, 110. Centre and below: The Sd.Kfz.9/2 in operation.

The Second Generation of Half-Tracked Vehicles

In the period 1932–7, considerable experience had been gained in the manufacture and operation of half-tracked vehicles. A new series incorporating improvements was therefore developed during 1937, when Adler of Frankfurt was given the task of producing light semi-tracks for a so-called standardised (Einheits) range. This range was given the prefix 'A' (for Adler), and some vehicles were actually completed in what was a parallel development to the 1-ton series by Demag. But no quantity production was undertaken and work on another new series was undertaken. (Some reference works confuse the 'A' series with the HK300 series— but the latter did not evolve until 1941, which was four years after the start of the 'A' series.)

Chronological development of the 'A' series was as follows:

1938 Adler A1. This was a light (3-tons fully laden) semi-track with a trailer capacity of just under half a ton. It was powered by a 65hp Maybach HL25 4-cylinder petrol engine, had hydraulic brakes, rubber-bushed suspension. Its top speed was 65 kph and it carried a crew of five.

1939 Adler A2. This vehicle was somewhat larger than the A1 but it weighed slightly less (2½-tons fully laden). It had a trailer capacity of two-thirds of a ton and was powered by a 78hp Maybach HL28 4-cylinder petrol engine. Apart from the use of torsion-bar suspension, it was automotively similar to the previous model. It carried six men and had a top speed of 65kph.

1939 Adler A3. This vehicle was almost identical to the A2 model, but it utilised the Maybach HL25 engine of the first model. It weighed 2¼-tons fully laden and had a top speed of 65kph. The trailer capacity was just under a ton.

1940 Adler A3F. This was a new version of the A3 equipped with a saloon-type body and powered by the Maybach HL28 engine of the A2. It weighed 3¼-tons fully laden, had a trailer capacity of 1-ton and a top speed of 75kph.

The next series was intended to be a standardised range with various load ratings intermediate between those of existing models, and it received the prefix 'HK' (Halb-Ketten, or half-track). The first figure in the designation denoted the trailer capacity in metric tons, and the remaining figures represented the project number. Work on the HK series began during 1939 but did not receive much enthusiasm because Hitler believed that the war would last no more than a couple of years, and that the existing range of vehicles would fulfil the needs of the army.

The HK series was as follows:

HK100: motor-cycle tractor, made by NSU Neckarsulm.
HK300: designed by Adler-Werke AG, Frankfurt.
HK600: shared between Hanomag and Demag.
HK900: Krauss-Maffei.
HK1600: Daimler-Benz.
HK2400: parent firm not finalised.
HK3500: parent firm not finalised.

Of these, only the motor-cycle tractor model HK100 was introduced into service (1940–1), where it rapidly acquired popularity.

HK 100 Series: Kleines Kettenkraftrad Sd.Kfz.2

This small motor-cycle tractor, designed by Wa.Prüf.6. was developed by NSU during 1939. It was intended mainly as a light air-portable tractor for towing the light guns and single-axle open supply trailers of paratroop and airborne units, but it was also used as a despatch vehicle in localities unsuitable for wheeled vehicles. It first saw action during the invasion of Crete.

The development of the Kettenkraftrad was based on the Motorkarette built by Austro-Daimler (later Steyr-Daimler-Puch) for the Austrian Army—which had steel tracks and lever-controlled steering and could be transformed into a wheeled vehicle by the manual application of pneumatic-tyred wheels to special axles provided on the chassis. By introducing steering brakes, reducing the track width and introducing the normal motor-cycle steering system at the front, NSU transformed the Austrian vehicle into one conforming to German military requirements. The prototype was designated Versuchs

Kfz.620; but when standardised the vehicle was classified as the Sd.Kfz.2 Kleines Kettenkraftrad, with the series project number HK100.

It entered service on 5th June 1941 and thereafter served mainly as a supply vehicle for rough terrain conditions. It remained in production until 1944. The mobility of the vehicle was as good as most tanks; and its ability as a light prime-mover, because of its wide gear selection, was very good. Production was shared between NSU in Neckarsulm and Stoewer in Stettin, and 8,345 were built in all. It was intended that production should also be taken over by Simca, but this never materialised.

Essentially, the vehicle retained the standard front wheel and handle-bars of a conventional motor-cycle but had two caterpillar tracks in place of the rear wheel. The front wheel steered the vehicle through slight angles, but controlled-differential steering brakes took over thereafter. The chassis was a box-like structure of pressed steel in two sections, welded together in a horizontal plane below the track guards. It contained the driving compartment, the engine and transverse seating accommodation for two men facing the rear. A hand-rail was provided on each side at the rear. The driver was seated on a saddle-seat directly above the transmission and clutch housing. Petrol tanks were mounted on each side and, together with the battery and tool compartments, made up the side walls of the vehicle. The engine was a centrally-mounted Opel Olympia 4-cylinder (positioned back-to-front) water-cooled petrol engine developing 37bhp. It was mounted behind the driver's seat and therefore could not be cooled by the slipstream, so it was cooled by a radiator with a shaft-driven fan coupled to the crankshaft at the rear. It drove the front sprockets through a transmission giving six forward gears and two reverse gears. The suspension consisted of two straddle-mounted, rubber-tyred bogie wheels on torsion-bars, a front driving sprocket and a rear idler. The inner bogie wheels were of the hollow spoked type, and the outer wheels were of the removable disc type. The tracks had 40 links each and were equipped with needle-bearings and replaceable rubber pads.

At a slightly later date, two cable-laying versions of this vehicle were introduced into service. They were:

Sd.Kfz.2/1 Kleines Kettenkraftrad für Feldfernkabel (light motor-cycle tractor for field telephone cable).

Sd.Kfz.2/2 Kleines Kettenkraftrad für Schweres Feldkabel (light motor-cycle tractor for heavy field cable).

Both vehicles had cable-drums mounted on frames behind the driver's seat.

A crane version was also produced in small numbers.

During 1941 NSU undertook a project for a heavier version of this vehicle with an increased load-carrying capacity and five seats (excluding the driver's). It weighed 2,250 kg, was powered by a 2-litre 4-cylinder Stump K20 engine developing 65hp, and was designated the HK102 (Grosses Kettenkraftrad). But it never progressed beyond the prototype stage.

A further engine was also being developed for the HK101, to replace the Opel. It was a 600cc 35hp (metric) 4-cylinder in-line short-stroke engine with a

kick-start. One interesting variant of this vehicle was the NSU Springer, which was used as a radio-controlled demolition vehicle.

Production of the Sd.Kfz.2 was as follows:

1941	1942	1943	1944
420	985	2,450	4,490

HK 300 Series

This series was developed by Adler during 1941 and represented an extension of the previous 'A' series. Like its predecessor, it was to have been a replacement for the 1-ton semi-tracked range. The prototype received the designation Kleine Zugmaschine HK301, and the first one was delivered to the army on 16th August 1941. In all, five trial vehicles were field tested and an order was placed for a pre-production series of fifty—but this order was never fulfilled. The HK301 was powered by a Maybach HL30 4-cylinder engine developing 95bhp. It had hydraulic steering brakes and mechanical road brakes. With a combat weight of 3.5 tons, it could carry eight men and achieve a maximum speed of 50mph.

A second vehicle, the HK305—which was to have had a Maybach HL42 6-cylinder 100hp engine, Maybach Olvar pre-selective transmission and pneumatic brakes—never passed the project stage.

HK 600 Series

Development of this vehicle—which was to be a substitute for both the 1-ton and 3-ton vehicles then in service—was shared between Hanomag and Demag. Two prototypes of unarmoured versions were built—HK601 and HK605—but other vehicles in the series were armoured. Development began during 1939 and was terminated during 1942. Hanomag built the HK601, and Demag built the HK605. These vehicles incorporated several advanced features—in particular, automatic transmission. Seven were under construction at Hanomag and thirty at Demag.

Chronological development was as follows:

1939 HK601 had a Maybach HL45Z 6-cylinder engine developing 120hp and Hanomag-Maybach pre-selective transmission. The steering brakes were hydraulic and the road brakes were pneumatic. The suspension was torsion-bar. The vehicle had a crew of eight men, weighed 6.3 tons fully laden, could carry 1½ tons and tow a maximum of 4½ tons. The maximum road speed was 47mph

1941 HK605 was partially armoured and was powered by a Maybach HL50 6-cylinder 170hp engine. The transmission was Maybach Olvar, and all the brakes were pneumatically operated Argus type. Suspension was torsion-bar. The vehicle had a trailer-load capacity of 4½ tons and a road speed of 48mph.

HK 900 Series

This series was developed by Krauss-Maffei AG, München, during 1940. As far as is known, only three unarmoured models were considered—the HK901, HK904 and the HK905. These vehicles were intended to replace both the 8-ton and 5-ton half-tracks. Thirty-four vehicles were ordered for delivery during the period

February to December 1941 but only thirty were completed—fifteen HK905 and fifteen HK901. The use of torsion-bar suspension was laid down in the basic conception of this series.

Chronological development was as follows:

1940 HK901 was powered by a Maybach HL45Z 6-cylinder engine developing 120hp. It had Maybach pre-selective transmission, mechanical road-brakes, pneumatic steering brakes, and torsion-bar suspension. Its laden weight was 11.5 tons and it had a trailer capacity of 8 tons. Its maximum speed was 47mph.

1941 HK904 was similar to the above with minor changes. It had a new HL66 180hp 6-cylinder engine.

1941 HK905 differed only in application of Olvar automatic transmission and simplified torsion-bar suspension.

HK 1600 Series

During 1940, Daimler-Benz of Berlin-Marienfelde undertook a project for the replacement of both the 12-ton and 18-ton semi-tracks. This was the HK1600 series. Only one model was produced, which appeared during 1941, and this was designated the HK1601. It was intended to power this vehicle by a 12-cylinder Maybach 10-litre engine developing 320hp, but the prototype employed a Maybach HL116 6-cylinder in-line engine developing 250hp. The vehicle could tow up to 16 tons and it had a maximum speed of 42mph. The transmission was of constant-mesh type, the steering brakes were hydraulic, the road brakes were pneumatic, the suspension was torsion-bar, and the laden weight was 16.2 tons. Four trial vehicles were built and thirty further vehicles were ordered for delivery during February 1941, under the designation HK1604. These were never completed.

Engines in the HK series were designed to provide a high degree of interchangeability. The 12- and 6-cylinder models, for example, were so designed that by using a conventional type of connecting-rod their crankshafts were interchangeable. Identical sodium-filled valves were to be used for both inlet and exhaust, and the bores and strokes were also standardised to enable interchange of pistons, etc.

In order to obtain increased engine power, modifications—including petrol injection—were carried out. This resulted in an improvement in peak engine power of 10% to 20% and a corresponding reduction in fuel consumption. And by changing heads it was possible to convert the engines from petrol to diesel. The ultimate aim of all these modifications was to simplify maintenance and production, to which end the following were standardised:

(a) Method of operation of every control.

(b) Method of each adjustment.

(c) The place where the adjustment was carried out.

(d) The location of each maintenance point.

A driver who had been trained on one of these vehicles was therefore competent to take over any other type without further instruction.

Modifications were effected in the design of the track shoes, which originally had to have a cut out portion for sprocket engagement. The new design overcame this by having engagement on the end of the pins.

The principal difference in the suspension was the change of bogie wheels, retaining the advantage of overlapping wheels but overcoming the troubles experienced with the interleaved wheels. This new type of wheel was made possible by the moving of the drive from the centre of the track to the outside edges.

The front axle suspension was modified and longitudinal torsion-bars were incorporated. The front axle itself was of tubular construction and the pivoting characteristics of the old type of suspension were retained.

The various vehicles in the HK series were intermediate in size between the corresponding standard models, the idea being to reduce the number of types. In practice, difficulty would have been experienced with the HK1601, which had a 16-ton trailed-load rating, as all gun loads, etc., had been designed for the existing 18-ton semi-tracked tractor. The projected heaviest military tractor was again to have had a trailed-load rating of 18 tons.

HK 2400 Series

At a conference between the army and Wa.Prüf.6 during 1941, suggestions were made for the introduction of a 24-ton semi-tracked vehicle with the designation HK2400. It is believed, however, that no work was done on this project.

HK 3500 Series

The final vehicle to be put forward in the HK series was the HK3500—a project for a vehicle to be built on the lines of a standard semi-track with a sheet-metal body resembling the Panther tank hull. The need for this vehicle arose because the 18-ton Sd.Kfz.9 recovery version was incapable of recovering Panther and Tiger tanks on its own. Upon consideration it was decided to use the Panther hull already in production, and the final outcome was the Panther recovery vehicle.

111. Above right: Adler A1 3-ton semi-track.
112. Below right: Front view of A1 semi-track.

113. **Above:** Nearside view of A2 2½-ton semi-track.
114. **Below:** Offside view of A2 semi-track.
115. **Above right:** Adler light semi-track model A3.
116. **Below right:** A3F semi-tracked staff car.

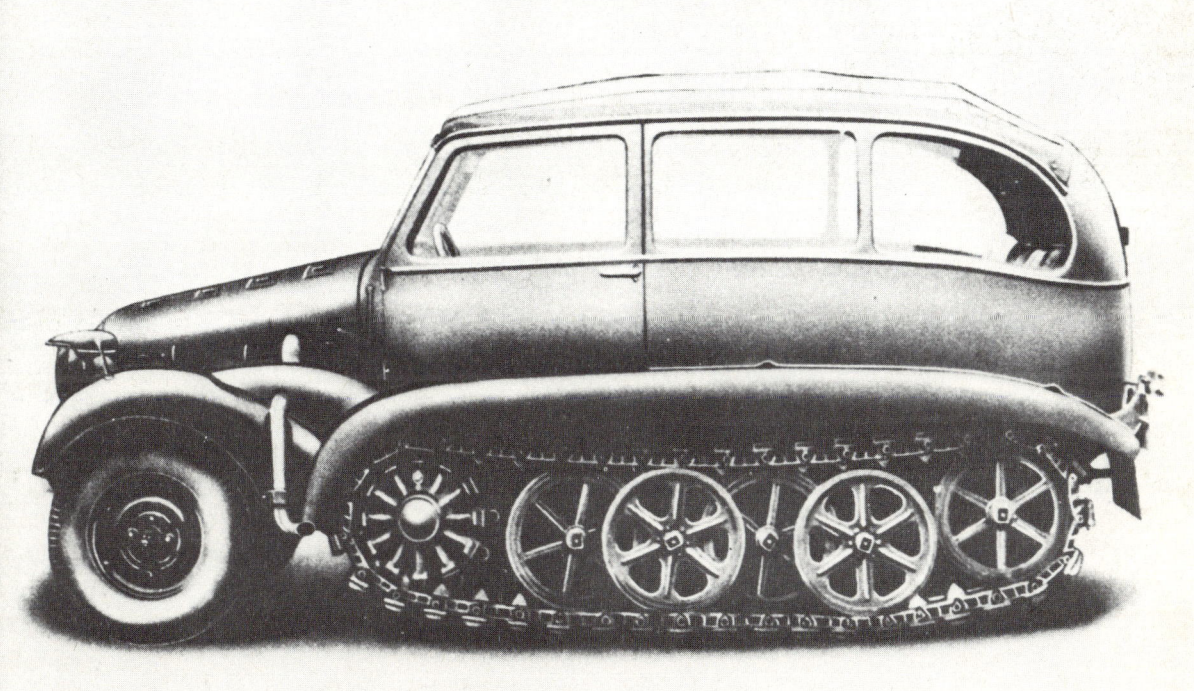

117, 118, 119, 120. General views of the HK-101 (Sd.Kfz.2) Kettenkraftrad motor-cycle tractor.

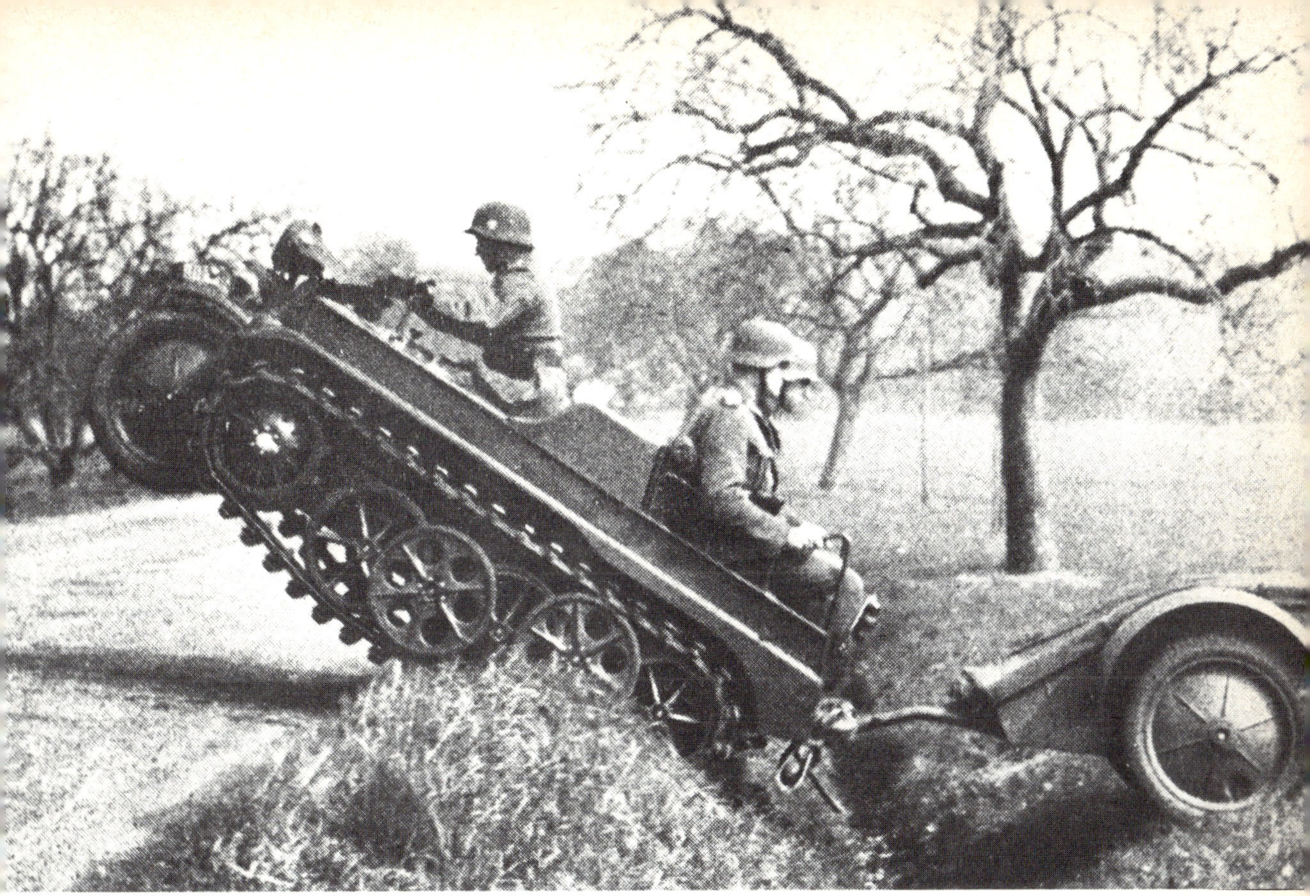

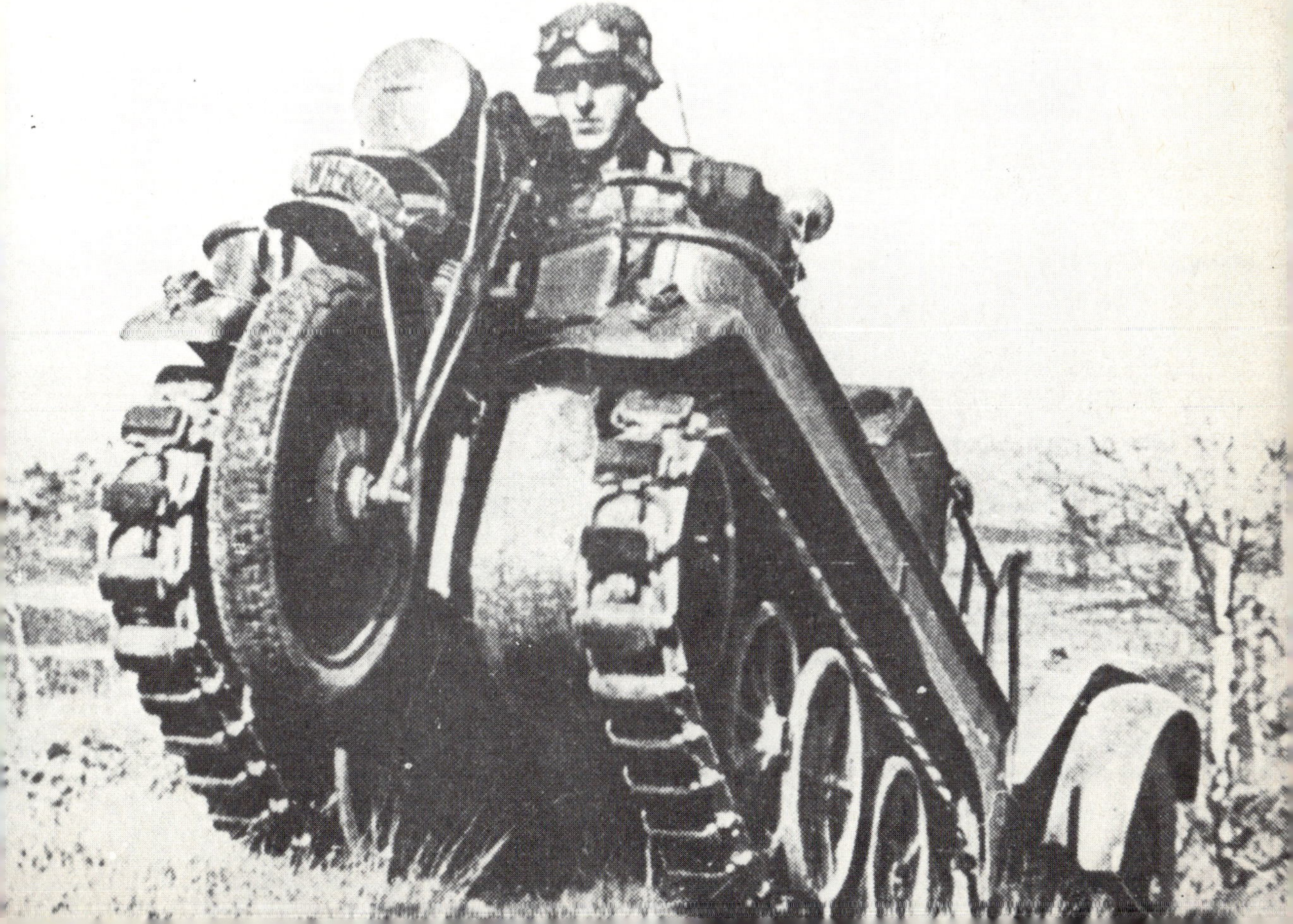

121. Left: HK-101 (Sd.Kfz.2).
122. Below left: Cut-away view of the HK-101 showing the automotive train.
123. Above right: Sd.Kfz.2/2 kleines Kettenkraftrad für schweres Feldkabel (light motor-cycle tractor for heavy field cable).
124. Below right: Sd.Kfz.2/1 kleines Kettenkraftrad für Feldfernkabel (light motor-cycle tractor for field telephone cable).

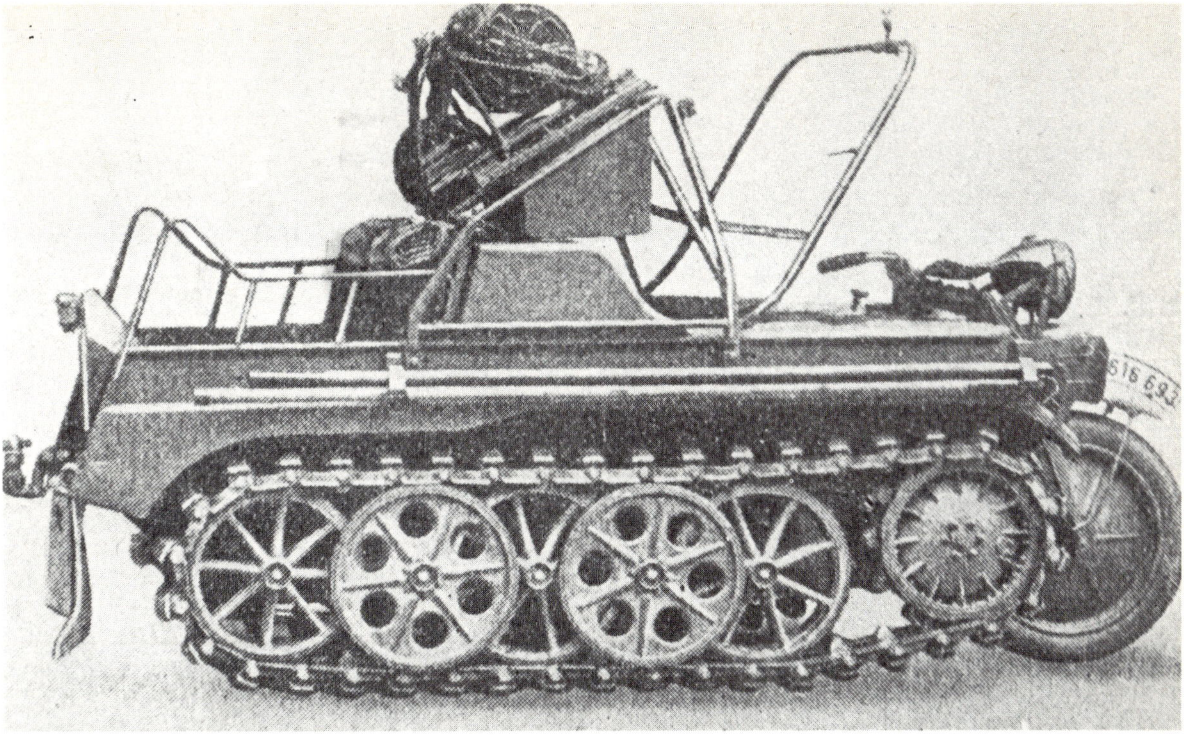

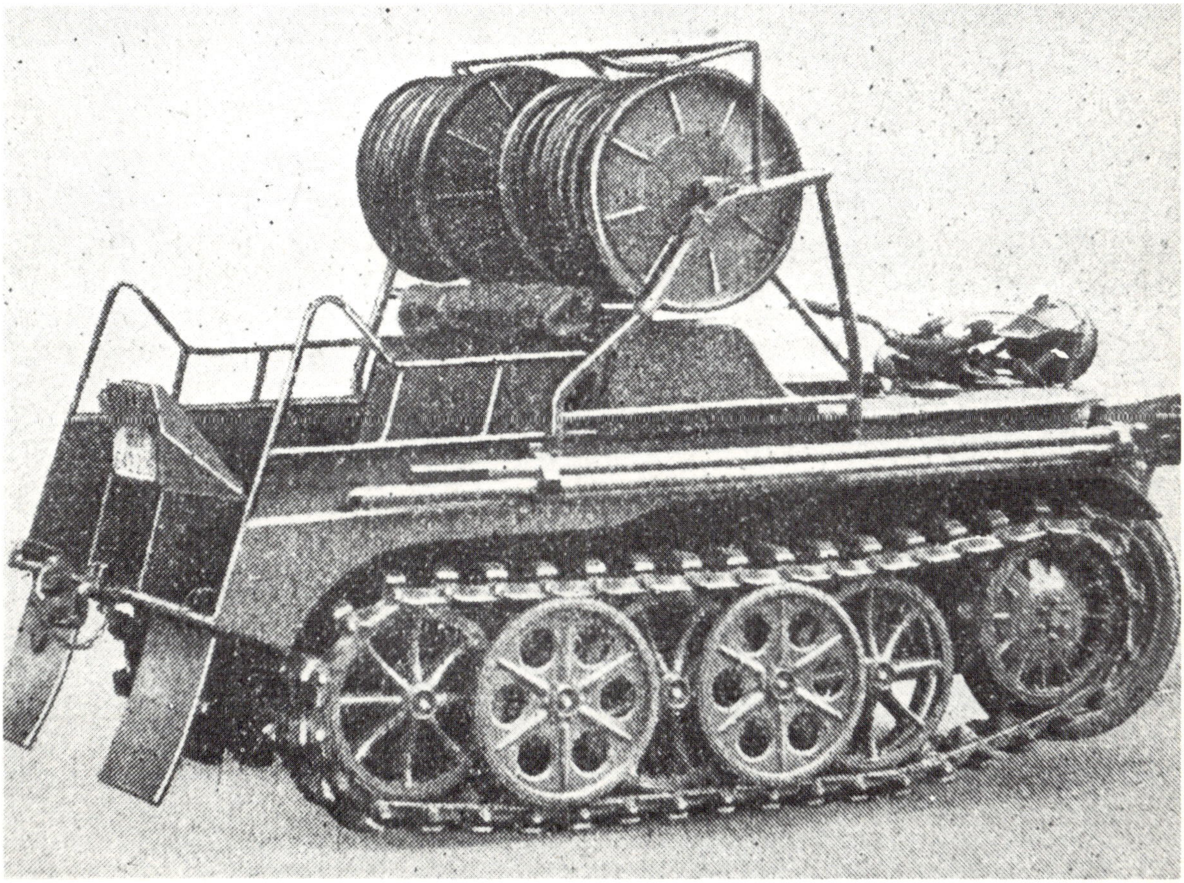

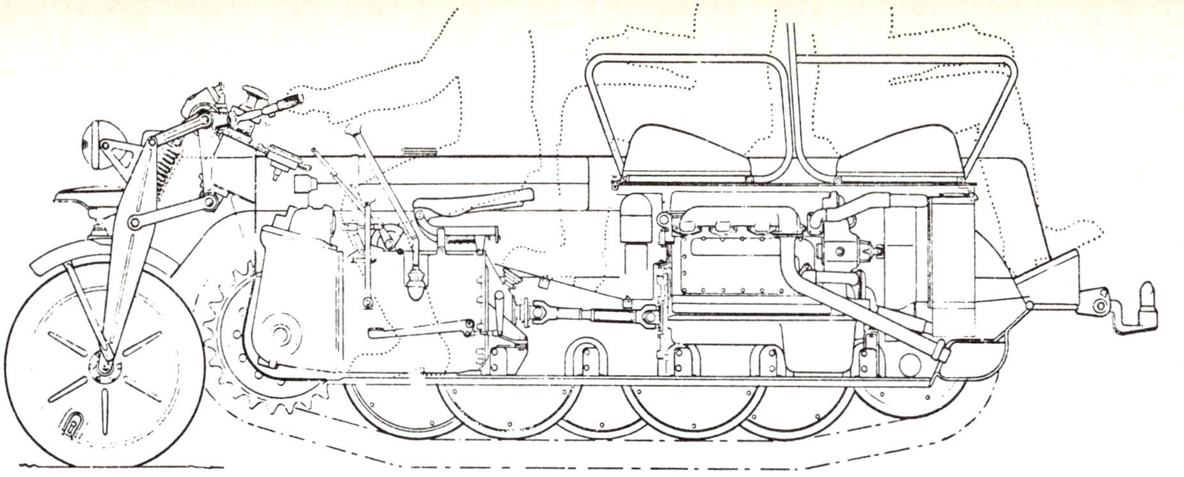

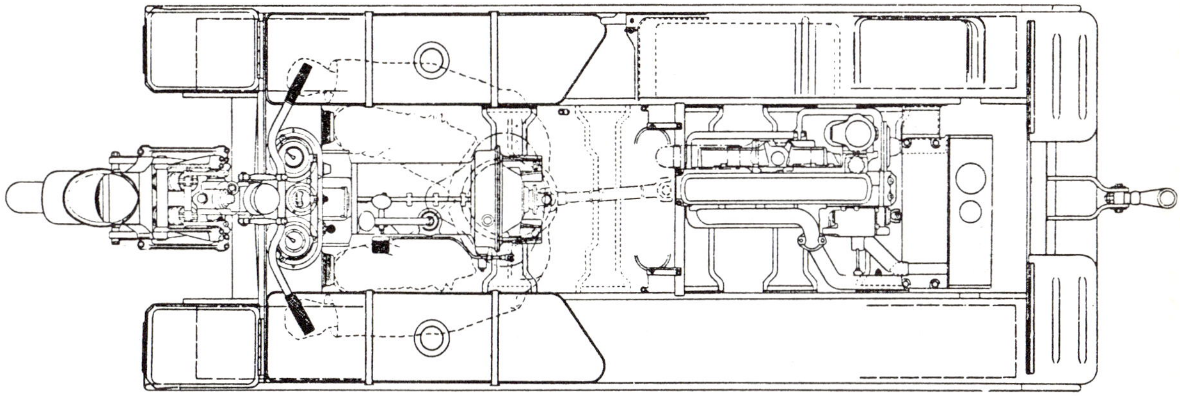

125. Above far left: The Sd.Kfz.2/2 in use by Luftwaffe troops.
126, 127. Above left and below: Early prototype of the HK-102 gros ses Kettenkraftrad (heavy motor-cycle tractor).
128. Above: General arrangement drawings of the HK-102.
129. Below: Final prototype of the HK-102. This vehicle never went into production.

130. Above: Experimental light semi-track model HK-301.
131. Below: Experimental light semi-track model HK-601.

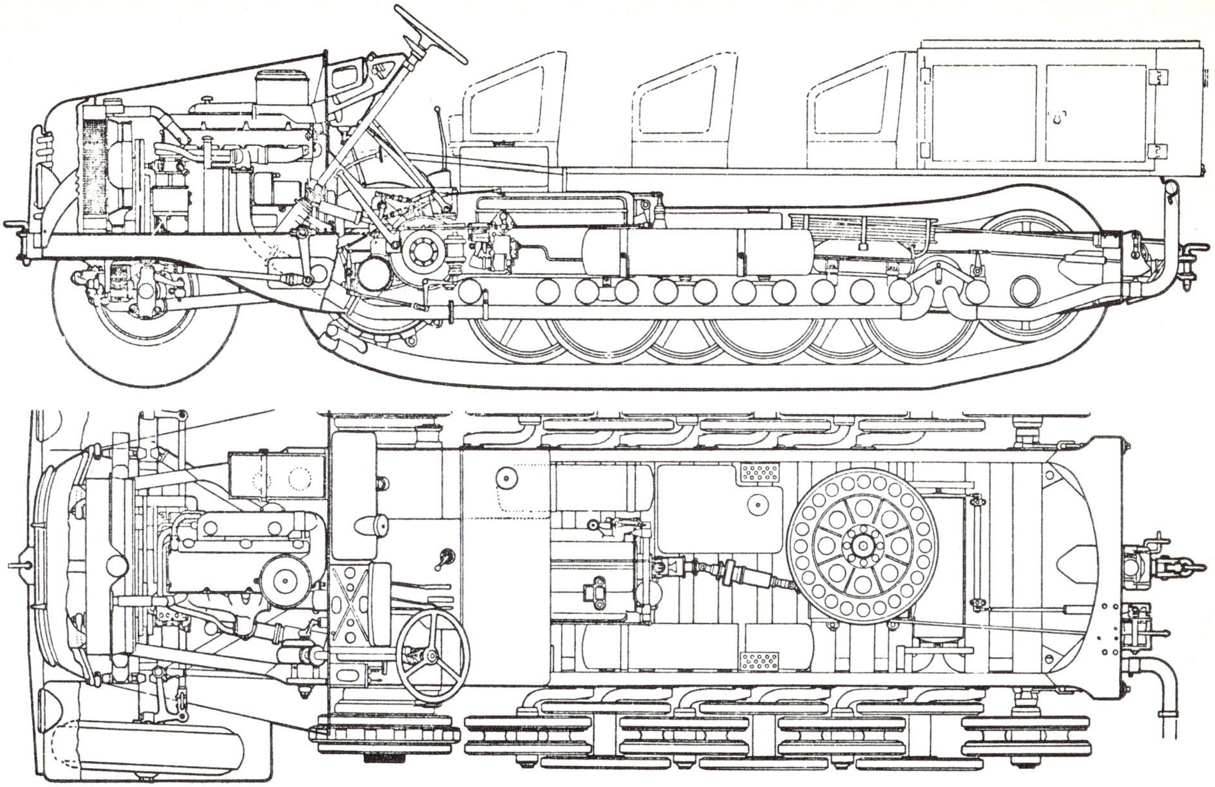

132. Above: General arrangement drawings of the HK-904 (the HK-901 was almost identical).
133. Below: Heavy experimental semi-track HK-1601.

The Third Generation of Half-Tracked Vehicles

It appears that the Germans recognised the need for both a fast and slow moving series in about 1942. During that year, under the personal direction of Hitler, a programme was launched for the introduction of a new series of semi-tracked load-carriers and tractors. One of the major concerns in their design was to make them more suited to operations in Russia. Although a fairly high degree of standardisation had been achieved in the previous models, the substantial losses in plant and material following Allied bombing raids necessitated further measures. Based upon service experience and also on knowledge gained in development of the HK series, which was apparently being continued but on a very much reduced scale, it was decided to produce a new series of vehicles. The factors influencing design were:

(a) The need for slow vehicles to tow the infantry gun.
(b) The fact that total capacity in production of needle roller-bearing track links had been reached.
(c) The need of the German Army for greater quantities of vehicles necessitating the overcoming of (b) and the simplification of production.

As a result of this a dry-pin track similar to the Panther track was produced.

The faster moving series was to be basically the same, but higher ratio gears and needle roller-bearing tracks would be fitted. The design of the sprockets, etc., accommodated this interchangeability and the dry-pin track was half the pitch of the needle roller track in order to reduce pin diameter and wear. The redesign of the needle roller track by extending the track pins and mounting rollers not only made this interchange possible but also made it possible to lubricate the bearings during assembly. The need for further lubrication during the rest of its life was thus eliminated. It was intended to use a steel-rimmed resilient wheel with the dry-pin track. But work on the fast-moving series never got off the ground.

The new low-speed tractors designated 'Wehrmacht Schleppers' (army tractors), were to be of simplified design and were to correspond to demands for such vehicles from all arms (artillery, infantry and ordnance), particularly the infantry. It was intended to dispense with the complicated technical design of previous half-tracks.

After drastic compromise, it was agreed that two models would be able to satisfactorily take over the roles then being filled by semi-tracks. The first was a light model—the Leichter Wehrmacht Schlepper (Le. WS)—and the second a heavier one, the Schwerer Wehrmacht Schlepper (S.WS). Only the latter, however, eventually entered production. Employed on both of these tractors were wider, all-steel, dry-pin tracks in place of the lubricated tracks with rubber blocks. Although these tracks reduced the overall speed, they provided a much higher tractive effort: the track pads gave good adhesion, especially on hard surfaces.

Apart from their engines, these vehicles were automotively similar. Both had sliding-mesh 4-speed gearboxes with transfer and Cletrac differentials. The steering and road brakes were pneumatic disc type, the latter with self-servo. The hand brakes acted mechanically on the road brakes. The suspension on the front wheels was transverse leaf type (except for the third prototype of the Le.WS) and that on the tracks was torsion-bar.

Production of these vehicles was scheduled to begin during Spring 1943.

The Le.WS

This was the lighter of the two vehicles and was an extension of the earlier HK300 series. It was intended that it should replace the 1-ton half-track, in particular, and all other light half-tracks then in service. Its design and development was in the hands of Adler-Werke of Frankfurt, who had been previously engaged on the HK300 programme, and development work followed an official order dated 7th May 1942.

This light all-purpose tractor, called the Locust, was able to tow up to 3 tons. It was lightly armoured and designed in such a way as to lend itself to the mounting of various types of weapons. The first two prototypes were completed towards the end of 1942 and were powered by Maybach HL30 4-cylinder engines developing 95hp. Production was scheduled for early 1943; but with the introduction of the RSO tracked lorry Hitler rejected this vehicle and no further development took place until 1944, when a third model appeared. This, the last to be developed, was based on the previous HK305 and was to have had a Maybach HL42 6-cylinder engine developing 100hp and torsion-bar suspension on both the front wheels and the track. It was never completed.

The S.WS

This vehicle was the only one of the series to enter production. On 27th July 1942 Hitler issued an order for the cancellation of the 5-ton Sd.Kfz.6 vehicle and for the turning over of production facilities for this vehicle to the output of the S.WS. The S.WS was a new, simplified, low-speed tractor designed primarily for use by infantry units as a supply vehicle in adverse conditions. The parent firm was Büssing NAG of Berlin-Oberschönweide, and Ringhöfer-Tatra assisted in production. On 27th July 1942 the OKH presented Wa.Prüf.6 with a requirement for 7,484 of these vehicles to be completed within the next two years. Production was scheduled to begin during the spring of 1943 with a monthly output of 150; but the first vehicles did not enter service until December 1943, when only five were completed. The firms assigned to producing these vehicles were Büssing NAG and Tatra in Czechoslovakia (the latter continuing production for some years after the war for the Czech Army). By September 1944 only 381 S.WS had been delivered to the army, and total production by 1945 amounted to 1,000. The Tatra version employed the air-cooled Tatra 111 engine.

The vehicle had a greatly simplified suspension and dry-pin tracks. It was mainly intended as a supply vehicle, although versions existed which had heavy bows for canvas covers and could carry wounded men (four stretchers, six minor casualties and two orderlies). There was also a version with an armoured cab which, apart from its role as a normal tractor, was used as a platform for various weapons. It was originally intended that the S.WS should replace the Maultier hybrid semi-tracks which had been produced as an expedient prior to its introduction; but as production never reached a satisfactory level, the Maultier remained in service for the remainder of the war.

The tractor was normally provided with an open lorry body. The engine was a 6-cylinder Maybach HL42 TRKMS, basically similar to and of the same rating as the engines used in the 1- and 3-ton tractors, and it had dry-sump forced lubrication, using a gear-type pump. The dry double-disc clutch, type PF220K, was the same as that used in the 1- and 3-ton tractors. The main gearbox, type Kb40D, gave four forward speeds and one reverse speed and was of sliding-mesh, non-synchromesh type. The auxiliary gearbox was connected to the main one by a short propeller shaft. Two ratios were provided. The vehicle had a conventional controlled differential. The steering brakes were mounted co-axially with the half-shafts and were pneumatically operated. Here the road brakes were not integral with

the driving sprockets. The half-shafts drove the driving sprockets through final reduction gears secured to each of the main chassis members. The suspension consisted of five pairs of double overlapping bogies, there being three widely spaced and two narrowly spaced on each side. The bogies were mounted on taper roller-bearings on hubs carried on radius arms, each separately sprung by means of a torsion-bar. The arrangement of these differed from that on the older semi-tracked vehicles in that the radius arms on the two sides were directed in opposite senses, those on the left pointing forward and those on the right trailing. Further, each torsion-bar was arranged to be co-axial (whereas in the older semi-tracks they were slightly offset) and tracks of the same number of links were used on each side. The driving sprocket consisted of two truncated cones, united at the smaller ends and carrying toothed rings bolted to the two outer rims. The bogies consisted of pairs of identical shallow discs carrying solid rubber tyres at their peripheries and were bolted to the hubs. They were detachable without removing the hubs. The idlers consisted of spoked wheels, rubber blocks being secured round their peripheries by steel clamping rings that also acted as guides for the teeth of the tracks. The idlers were mounted on cranked axles and the usual track-tensioning device was used, comprising a nut and threaded rod device incorporating a shear-bolt. Each track consisted of fifty-five main links, each carrying two spuds and two guide teeth, and an equal number of intermediate links hinged together by track pins. The intermediate links were secured on the outer side by a head and on the inner side by a circlip and pin. The guide teeth ran between the widely-spaced bogies but outside the narrowly-spaced ones. The track width was 500mm (19.7in).

The front wheel steering was of the ZF Ross worm-and-cam type, and it was connected with a pneumatic valve for operating the track brakes when the steering wheel had been turned through a certain angle. A new feature was a lever on the dashboard that enabled each track to be braked independently, allowing the vehicle to be driven on one track only in the event of one track slipping excessively or when removing tracks.

A winch was optional and would be incorporated only by special request. It was driven from the auxiliary gearbox through a propeller shaft and worm gear. The capacity of the winch was 5 tons.

The version with an armoured cab weighed 10.5-tons unladen and could carry up to 3½ tons. The trailer load capacity was 8 tons. In this version the engine, radiator and driver's compartment were enclosed in light armour plate. This armour was joined by welding except that of the engine cover, which was bolted on. The armour varied from 16mm on the front to 8mm on the sides and roof. The body of the vehicle consisted of a flat bed covered with steel plates and fitted with hinged sides. A compartment of the same height as the sides extended across the rear of the body. A seat for a gun crew was located at the back of the cab and was protected by an extension of the side armour. A folding canvas top was provided. This armoured version was not fitted with a winch.

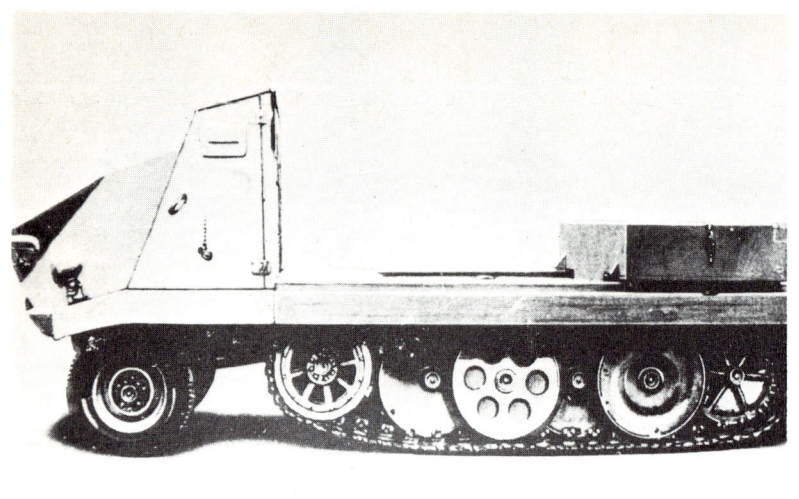

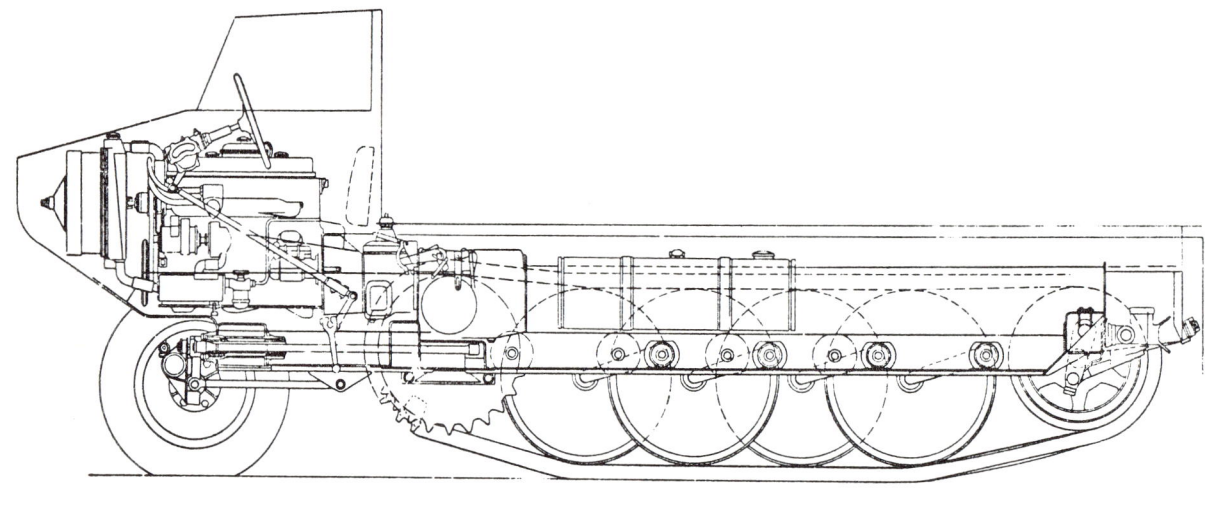

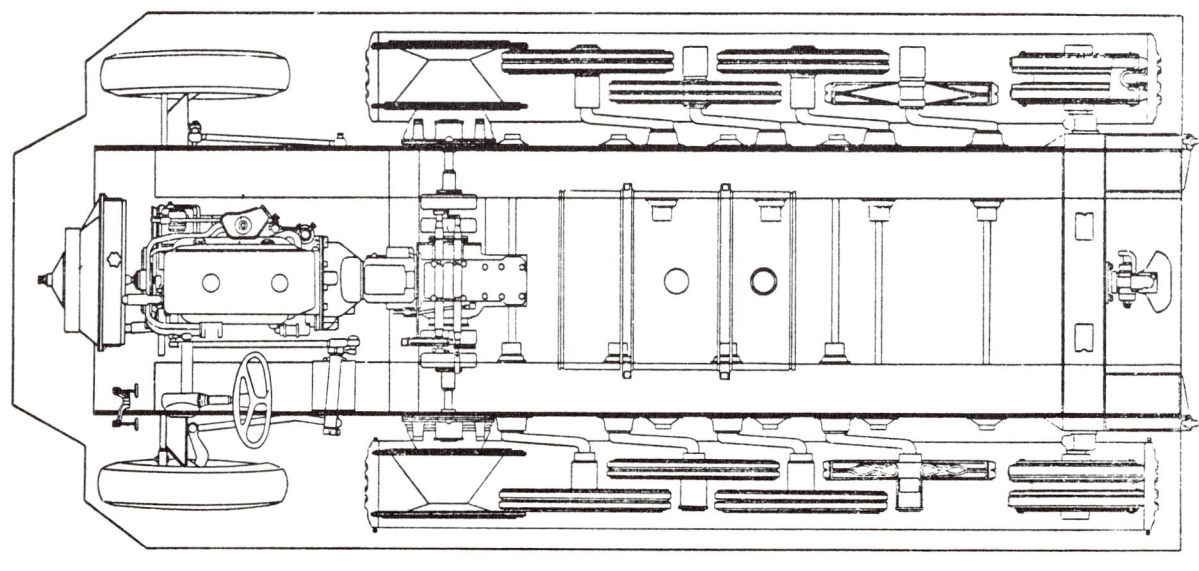

134. **Above left:** First prototype of the light military tractor Le.WS.
135. **Above centre:** Second prototype of the Le.WS.
136. **Above right:** Heavy military tractor s.WS.
137. **Below far left:** General arrangement drawings of the projected third model of the Le.WS.
138. **Centre Left:** Offside view of s.WS.
139. **Below left:** Three-quarter rear view of s.WS.

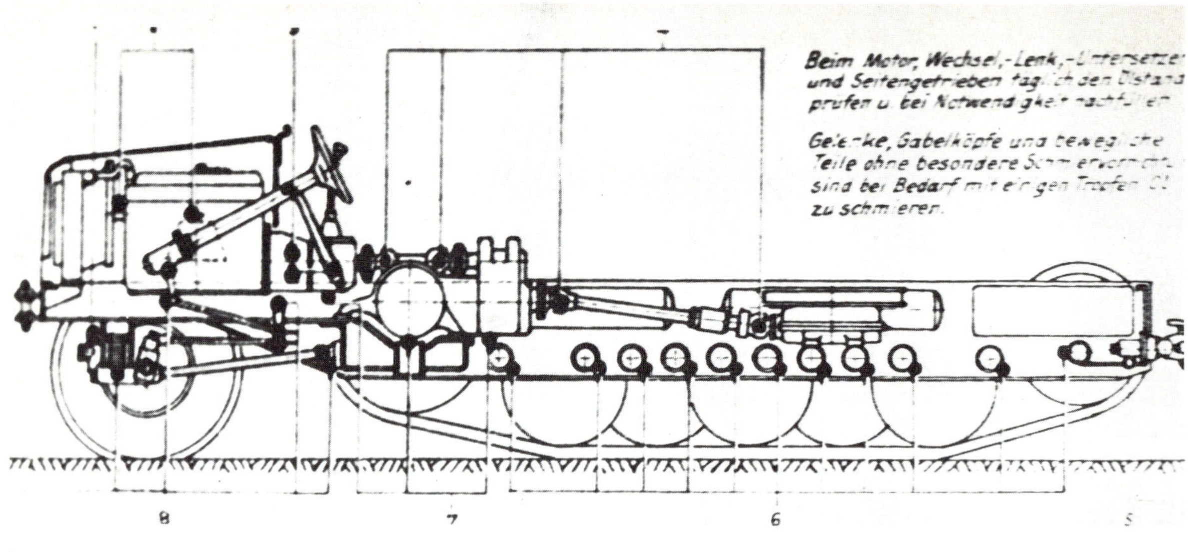

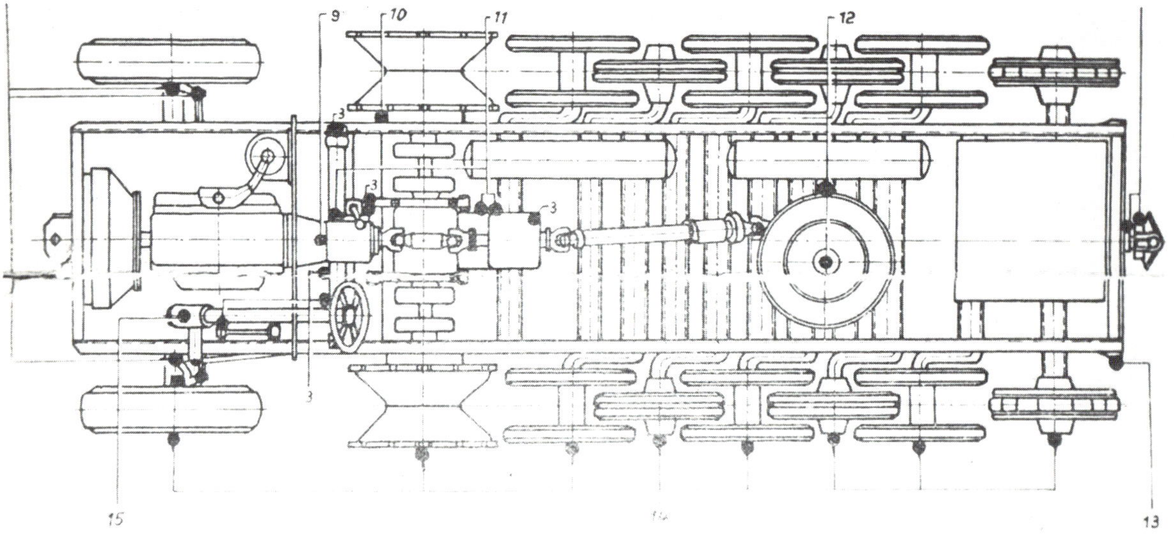

Beim Motor, Wechsel-, Lenk-, Untersetze... und Seitengetrieben täglich den Ölstand prüfen u. bei Notwendigkeit nachfüllen.

Gelenke, Gabelköpfe und bewegliche Teile ohne besondere Schmiervorricht... sind bei Bedarf mit einigen Tropfen Öl zu schmieren.

8   7   6   5

9   10   11   12

15   13

140, 141. Above:
General arrangement drawings of the s.WS.
142. Below: Heavy military tractor s.WS with armoured cab.

Maultiers (Mules)

Maultiers were medium cross-country lorries with semi-tracked suspension systems, and they were introduced as an expedient pending the adoption of the Wehrmacht Schleppers (Le.WS and S.WS). As a result of their experiences in Russia, the Germans felt the need for a semi-tracked load-carrying vehicle since ordinary wheeled transport became immobilised under certain mud and snow conditions.

In contrast to half-tracks, which were rated by their trailer capacity, these vehicles were classified according to their payload. The development of a tracked suspension conversion unit for application to ordinary lorry chassis was therefore undertaken, this being considered the most economical means of dealing with the problem. And although these vehicles were regarded as improvisations, they do appear to have fulfilled a definite requirement with reasonable success.

The original Maultier was produced by the SS Division 'Das Reich', who fitted a Ford V8 lorry with the tracked system taken from an English Carden-Loyd tractor captured at Dunkirk. This conversion was carried out in the field. The idea was taken further by higher authorities, who sanctioned production of the vehicle—including the original British running gear. The resulting Maultiers (mules), as they were colloquially called, were rated according to their payload; but where standard lorries were modified, the payload was reduced.

The first model to be adopted was the 2-ton m.gl.Lkw (mittlerer gleisketten Lastkraftwagen 2t, or medium tracked lorry, 2-ton), which was used in both North Africa and Russia. In vehicle establishments of certain anti-tank units it replaced some of the light semi-tracked $1\frac{1}{2}$-ton vehicles (Sd.Kfz.10) and ammunition trailers (Sd.Ah.31), probably because of its increased payload capacity without considerable sacrifice in cross-country performance.

The payload of these vericles was reduced from 3 tons in the 4-wheeled version to 2 tons due to the weight of the track unit and the fact that the vehicle was not well suited for load-carrying purposes. All semi-tracked lorries (2 tons) were classified as Sd.Kfz.3. Basic vehicles converted were the 3-ton models by Opel, Ford and Magirus (Klöckner-Humboldt-Deutz). In 1942 the Opel model was the first to be developed, and the Ford and KHD models went into production during December 1942. Ford vehicles were classified as V3000S/SSM (m.gl.Lkw.2t Maultier Ford, Sd.Kfz.3b), those by KHD as S3000/SSM (m.gl.Lkw.2t Maultier KHD, Sd.Kfz.3c), and those by Opel as 3.6–36S/SSM (m.gl.Lkw. 2t Maultier Opel, Sd.Kfz.3a). Other 3-ton tracked lorries employed were the Klöckner 3-ton tracked lorry type 33G1, the Henschel 3-ton tracked lorry type 33D1 and the Mercedes-Benz 3-ton tracked lorry type LGF3000.

The Ford vehicles were built by the factory in Cologne and also in Amsterdam and Asnières, France. (Ford assembled 1,000 Maultier half-track conversions to their lorries at Asnières). The Opel-Blitz version was built at Opel's Brandenburg/Havel plant. In all, Opel built 4,000 chassis (excluding 300 chassis for the Panzerwerfer 42), Ford 13,952 and Klöckner-Humboldt-Deutz 2,500. The best of these were the diesel-engined KHD and the Opel-Blitz models, but they were few in number. All production models were fitted with the SSM track system, although experiments were carried out with various types of suspension. The SSM track system was a suspension unit of Carden-Loyd type designed by the Waffen-SS, using an all-steel dry-pin track similar to that of the Pz.Kpfw.I light tank. It could be built on to the standard 3-ton lorry by removing the rear wheels and associated parts and fitting a shortened propeller shaft.

Apart from the basic open load-carrying version, an ambulance version was introduced (designated Sd.Kfz. 3/4) and also a box-body version for general use. The most numerous models were those by Ford and Opel. They were not very highly regarded, however, because of their high-speed petrol engines, which proved unsuitable for semi-tracked vehicles. The KHD version, with its low-speed Deutz diesel, was much more successful but was available only in relatively small numbers. Only the Ford model was retained in the 1944 von Schell

Programme, and production of even this vehicle was terminated in May of that year.

A second Maultier class appeared during 1943, based on the Mercedes-Benz L4500R lorry and having a 4½-ton payload capacity. It was introduced as a stop-gap following a decision to discontinue production of the 5-ton Sd.Kfz.6, and pending the introduction of the S.WS (sometimes written as SWS). Even so, it was retained in the 1944 programme. It was designated m.gl.Lkw. 4½t offen Maultier (mittlerer gleisketten Lastkraftwagen 4½t). (Later, the 'm' was changed to 's' for 'schweres'.) The Sd.Kfz. number of this vehicle was originally 4, but during the later reclassification it received the new designation Sd.Kfz.3/5 (the vehicle now being called the L4500S).

The suspension of this vehicle differed from that used on the 2-ton Maultier, closely resembling that on the Pz.Kpfw.II light tank. There were five bogie wheels on each side, each mounted on one arm of a bell-crank lever—the other arm carrying a quarter-elliptic leaf spring which bore against a stop at its other end. There were three small unevenly-spaced return rollers. The front driving sprocket and idler were somewhat smaller than those on the Pz.Kpfw.II. The front wheels were steered by a steering wheel in the normal manner. Track braking was effected by separate hand levers. The weight of the vehicle was about 8.2 tons empty, and the payload capacity was 4.5 tons. A recovery version also existed.

In all, 1,480 of the 4½-ton model were built at the Daimler-Benz factory at Gaggenau.

2-ton Sd.Kfz.3

In the Opel version the chassis, body and engine were those of the normal Opel 3.6–36S 3-ton lorry (4 × 2). The drive was taken in the normal way from the clutch and gearbox by a propeller shaft that had been shortened so that the differential lay under the rear of the driving cab. From the differential, the drive was taken by half-shafts, through brakes, to the sprockets.

The rear brakes were located just inside the sprockets and were operated hydraulically, together with the front brakes, by the footbrake. There were two handbrake levers mounted one on each side of the gearbox casing, each operating by cable the rear brake on that side. The track system was very similar to the Horstmann slow-motion track used on British carriers and had certain features in common with those of the old British light tank Mk. VI. The driving sprocket was ring-mounted on the chassis frame; and the idler wheel was at the rear. The bogie wheels were mounted in pairs in two bogie brackets, each of which also carried one of the two return rollers. In each bogie bracket assembly the inner bogie wheel and the return roller were carried in forks that formed two arms of a T-shaped bracket, and the third arm was the bearing by which the assembly was carried on the auxiliary frame. Just below the bearing was pivoted the secondary fork carrying the second bogie wheel unit. Between cups on the end of the secondary fork and extensions on the T-shaped bracket, just below the return roller, were twin 'chatter' springs mounted on guide rods. These springs controlled the

relative movements of the two bogies in that bogie assembly. Bogies and return rollers were rubber-tyred.

The track consisted of all-metal links, each link having two tongues between which the bogie wheels passed. The idler wheel was mounted at the centre of an arm which was pivoted at the top and bolted at its lower end to one of several holes in a quadrant on an auxiliary frame.

The track system was mounted beneath the chassis frame on a bed-shaped auxiliary frame consisting of tubular side- and cross-members. The two centre cross-members formed the axles upon which the bogie bracket assemblies were mounted, and the rear cross-members supported the idler wheel.

The Ford 2-ton Maultier V3000S/SSM (Sd.Kfz.3b) had a Ford (side-valve) petrol V8 engine developing 95hp. The transmission was Ford sliding mesh. Apart from slight dimensional variations, the vehicle was otherwise automotively similar to the Opel vehicle.

The KHD 2-ton Maultier S3000/SSM (Sd.Kfz.3c) had a Deutz KH-D diesel 4-cylinder engine developing 80hp. The transmission was ZF sliding mesh. The vehicle was otherwise automotively similar to the previous types.

The Mercedes-Benz 4½-ton Maultier (Sd.Kfz.3/5) had a Mercedes-Benz diesel 6-cylinder developing 112hp. The transmission was ZF sliding mesh and there were other slight differences in automotive layout.

Maultier Production was as follows:

	1942	1943	1944	Total
3-ton model ...	1,635	13,000	7,310	21,945
4½-ton model ...	—	594	886	1,480

143. Above right: Opel 3.6-36S/SSM 2-ton Maultier, Sd.Kfz.3a.
144. Centre right: Chassis of Opel Maultier (Sd.Kfz.3a).
145. Below right: Drawing showing the tracked Maultier system as fitted to the 3-ton conversions.

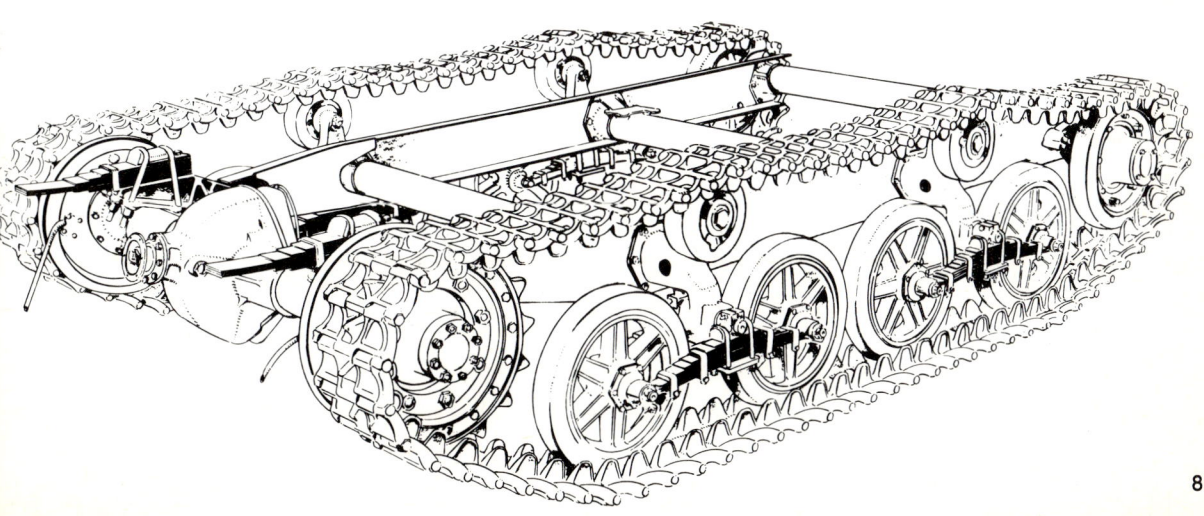

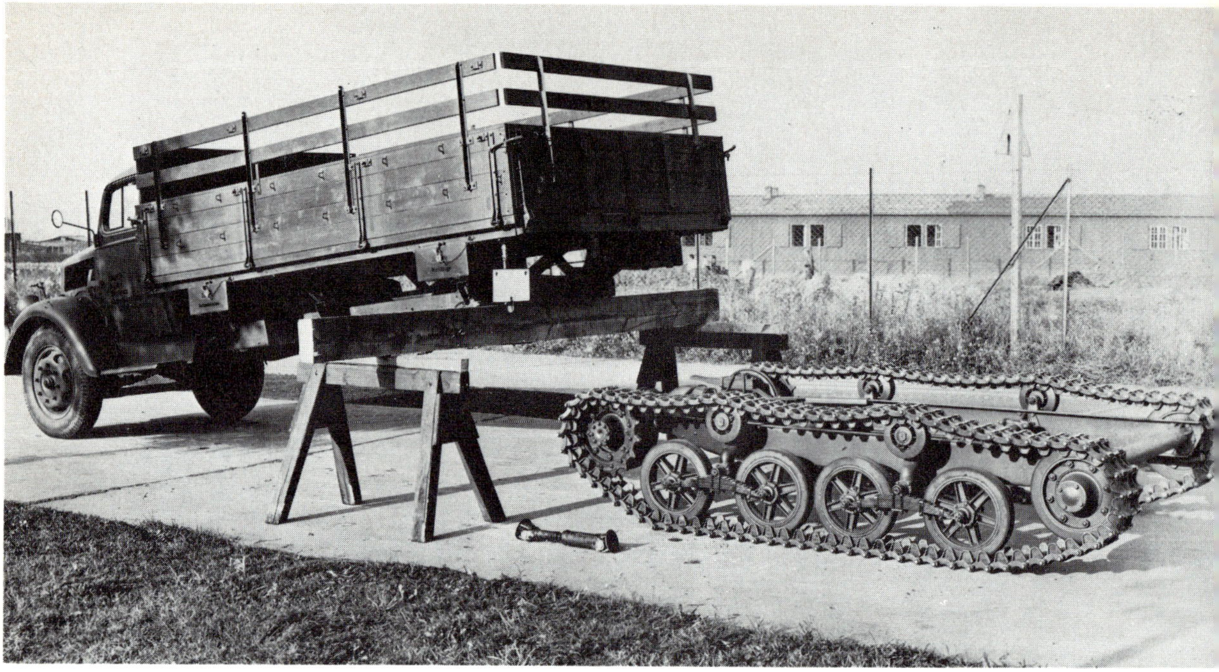

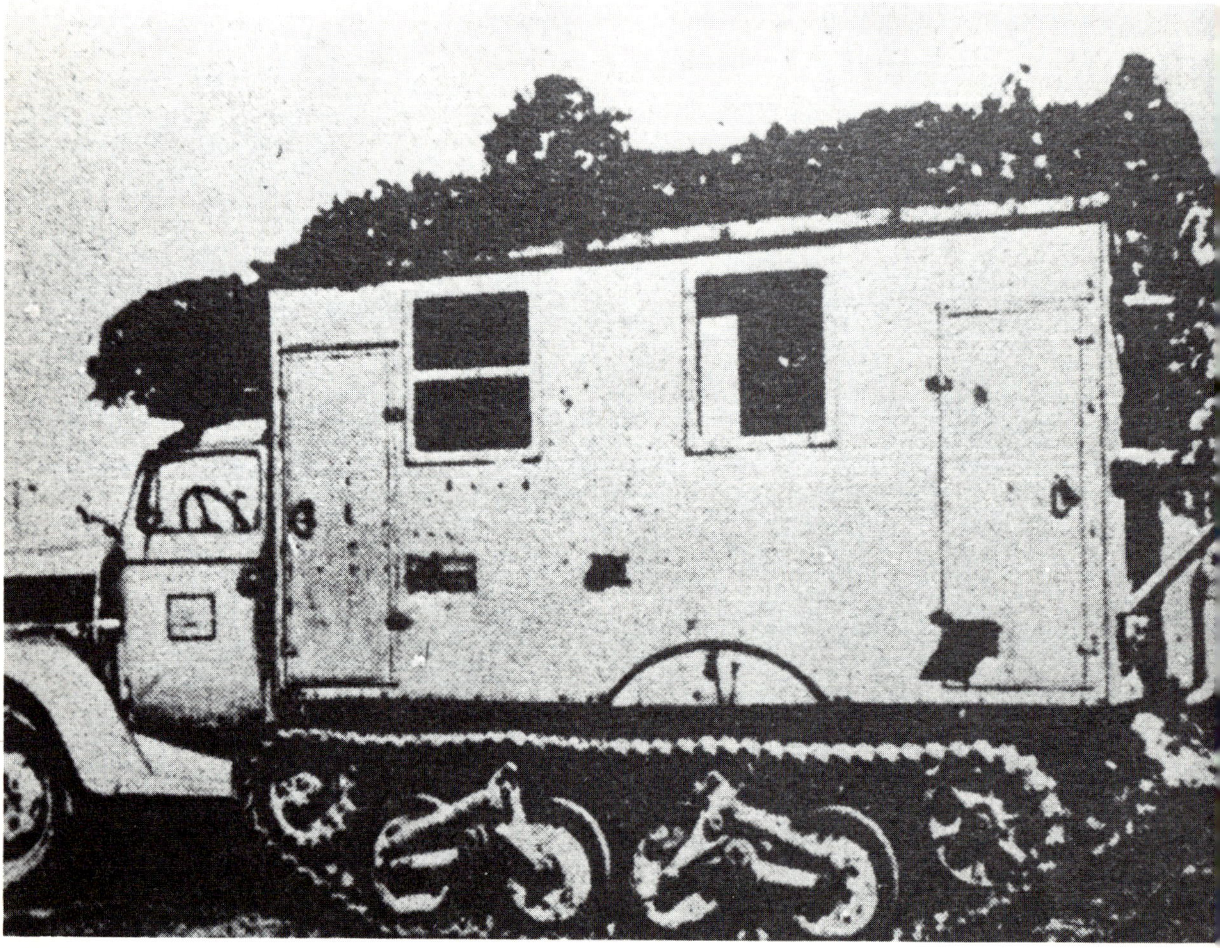

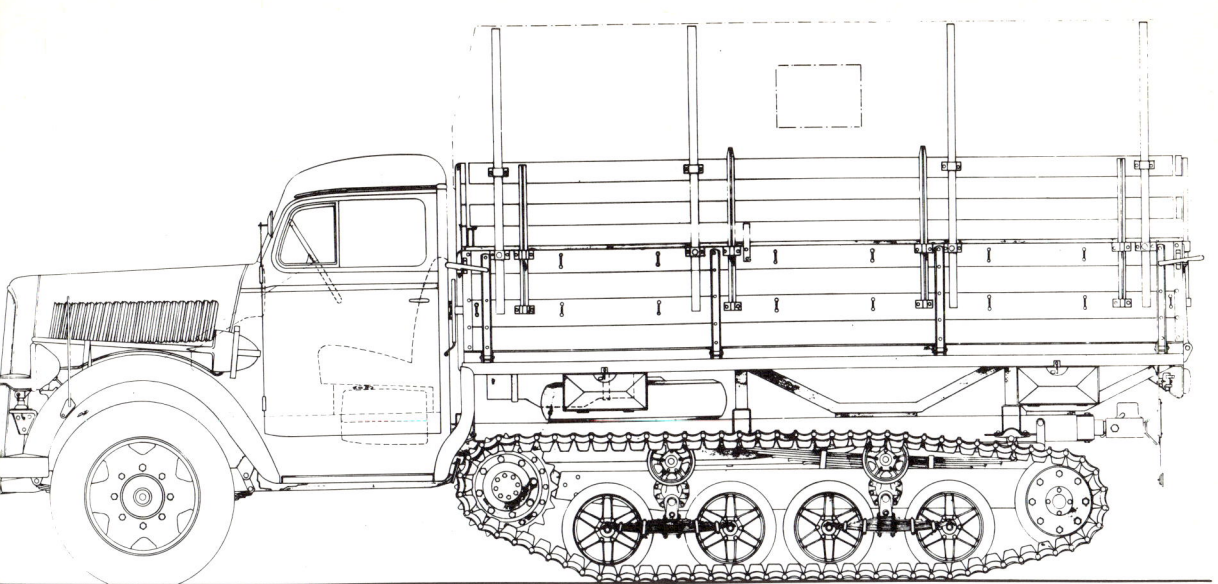

146. Left: Maultier track section being maintained after removal from an Opel Sd.Kfz.3a.
147. Above: General arrangement drawing of the Opel Sd.Kfz.3a.
148, 149. Below left and right: A special conversion of the Maultier (Opel Sd.Kfz.3a) used to accompany V-2 missile sites.

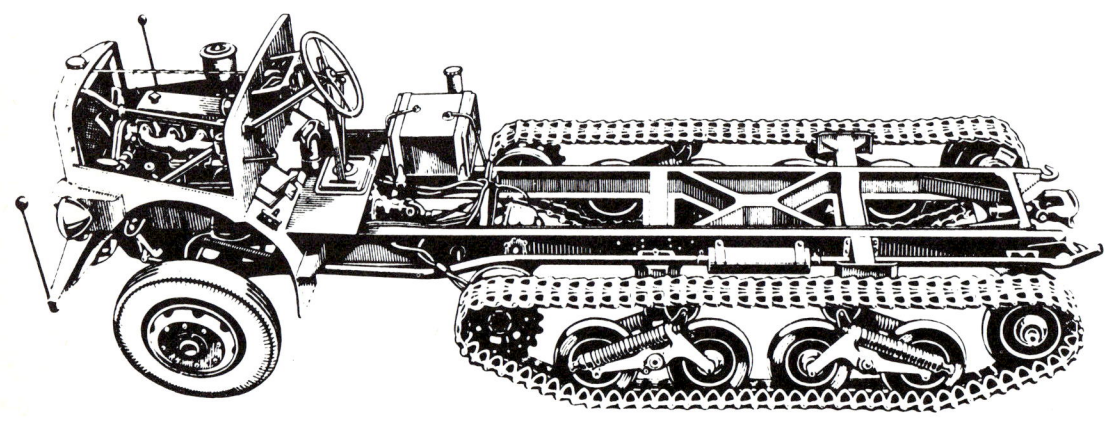

150. Above: Ford V3000S/SSM 2-ton Maultier (Sd.Kfz.3b).
151. Above right: Klöckner-Humboldt-Deutz (Magirus) S3000/SSM 2-ton Maultier (Sd.Kfz.3c).
152. Below: The automotive layout of the KHD Maultier.
153. Right: Mercedes-Benz 3-ton tracked lorry (modified from LGF-3000). The suspension system on this vehicle is slightly different from the other models.

154. Left: Mercedes-Benz s.gl.Lkw. 4½-ton offen Maultier (Sd.Kfz.3/5).
155. Centre: Offside view of the Mercedes-Benz 4½-ton Maultier.
156. Below: Three-quarter rear view of the Mercedes-Benz 4½-ton Maultier.

Appendices

1: SPECIAL CHEMICAL WARFARE ADAPTATIONS OF HALF-TRACKED VEHICLES

A series of special vehicles for smoke and chemical warfare was produced. Most of these equipments were built on the chassis of the 1-ton and 3-ton semi-tracked vehicles.

Gasspührkraftwagen (gas-detection vehicle) Sd.Kfz.10/1

This was very little different from the standard light semi-tracked vehicle 1-ton Sd.Kfz.10 and was, indeed that vehicle fitted out to carry personnel of the gas scout section and their equipment. The crew consisted of seven men in addition to the driver.

Chassis: light semi-tracked vehicle 1-ton, Sd.Kfz.10
Length, overall: 15ft 6in
Width, overall: 6ft 0in
Height, overall: 5ft 4in
Combat weight: 4.9 tons

Entgiftungskraftwagen (decontamination vehicles)

Light and medium decontamination vehicles existed, again built on 1-ton and 3-ton semi-tracked vehicle chassis respectively. In both cases the equipment carried a dispensing hopper at the rear, driven by the road wheels, by which the decontaminant was distributed over the road or terrain requiring treatment. Between the driver's compartment and the hopper, eight large drums of bleach were stacked for use in the latter. In addition to this, each vehicle carried sixteen decontamination canisters, each holding 22lb of decontaminant for use by hand on isolated areas. The crew of each vehicle was three, in addition to the driver.

Leichter Entgiftungskraftwagen (light decontamination vehicle) Sd.Kfz.10/2
Chassis: light semi-tracked vehicle 1-ton, Sd.Kfz.10
Length, overall: 15ft 7in
Width, overall: 6ft 1in

Combat weight: 4.8 tons   Height, overall: 5ft 4in
Mittlerer Entgiftungskraftwagen (medium decontamination vehicle) Sd.Kfz.11/2
Chassis: light semi-tracked vehicle 3-ton, Sd.Kfz.11
Length, overall: 19ft 0in
Width, overall: 6ft 7in
Height, overall: 7ft 10in
Combat weight: 6.7 tons

The medium equipment carried 760kg (1676lb) of bleach and could decontaminate a strip 5ft 3in wide and 1 mile long.

Sprühkraftwagen (bulk contamination vehicles)

The Germans developed two vehicles that formed part of the equipment of contamination batteries. Both had a crew of one in addition to the driver. The spray was operated from a panel behind the driver's compartment and emitted from a jet on a swivelling arm at the top of the vehicle, the muzzle being fed by a flexible hose of small diameter hung on support arms. The nozzle traversed in an arc, which enabled a wide zone to be sprayed.

Leichter Sprühkraftwagen (light bulk contamination vehicle) Sd.Kfz.10/3
Chassis: light semi-tracked vehicle 1-ton, Sd.Kfz.10
Length, overall: 15ft 6in
Width, overall: 6ft 4in
Height, overall: 5ft 9in
Combat weight: 4.5 tons
Load capacity: 1,760lbs of blister gas
Operating speed: 5mph
Mittlerer Sprühkraftwagen (medium bulk contamination vehicle) Sd.Kfz.11/3
Chassis: light semi-tracked vehicle, 3-ton, Sd.Kfz.11
Length, overall: 18ft 2in
Width, overall: 6ft 7in
Height, overall: 6ft 11in
Combat weight: 7.3 tons
Load capacity: 2,500 lbs of blister gas
Operating speed: 5mph

Nebelkraftwagen (smoke vehicle) Sd.Kfz.11/1

In this vehicle a large part of the body was taken up by racks for smoke thermal generators or other munitions. Chassis: light semi-tracked vehicle 3-ton, Sd.Kfz.11
Length, overall: 23ft 7in
Width, overall: 8ft 2in
Height, overall: 8ft 10in
Combat weight: 7.3 tons

2: MANUFACTURERS ENGAGED IN THE PRODUCTION OF HALF-TRACKED VEHICLES

Engines only

Maybach, Friedmichshafen.
Niederschönweide (Nordbau), Berlin.

Vehicles only

Carl F. W. Borgward (formerly Hansa-Lloyd), Bremen.
Büssing NAG, Braunschweig; Elbing; Leipzig; Berlin-Oberschöneweide.
Demag, Wetter/Ruhr; Duisberg.
Daimler-Benz, Unterturkheim; Gaggenau; Mannheim; Berlin-Marienfelde.

Famo GmbH, Breslau.
Hanomag, Hannover-Linden.
Krupp, Essen; Bochum; Magdeburg-Buckau.
Mechanische Werke, Cottbus.
Mühlen und Industrie AG, Braunschweig.
Maschinenfabrik Niedersachsen, Hannover-Wulfel.
Skoda, Pilsen; Prague.
Vomag, Plauen.

Complete vehicles and some Maybach engines under licence

Adler, Frankfurt/Main.
Krauss-Maffei, München.
Saurer, Vienna.

3: AIDS TO SNOW-CROSSING PERFORMANCE

Experiments were carried out at St. Johann in 1944–5 to improve the snow-crossing performance of the original semi-track series. This was accomplished firstly by fitting wedge-shaped track extensions that doubled the width of the track, and secondly by the introduction of a boat-shaped ski 'Mittelkufe 44' that was fitted to the front of

5: TECHNICAL DATA TABLES

1-ton half-track Sd.Kfz.10 series

			D 11 1	D 11 2	D 11 3	D4	D6
Original Manufacturer	...	...	Demag	Demag	Demag	Demag	Demag
Sd.Kfz. No.	...	...	Nil	Nil	Nil	Nil	10
Weight, unladen (tons)	...	...	N.K.	1.90	2.40	2.75	2.85
Weight, laden (tons)	...	...	N.K.	2.56	3.40	3.75	3.85
Trailer load (tons) ...	...	...	N.K.	0.60	0.60	0.60	0.60
Length, o.a. (feet)	...	...	N.K.	10.95	14.5	15.6	15.4
Width, o.a. (feet) ...	...	...	N.K.	5.28	5.94	6.26	6.00
Height, o.a. (feet) ...	...	...	N.K.	5.28	5.62	5.78	5.78
Wheel centres (feet)	...	...	N.K.	N.K.	N.K.	N.K.	5.38
Track centres (feet)	...	...	N.K.	N.K.	N.K.	N.K.	4.95
Ground contact, tracks (feet)	...	...	N.K.	N.K.	N.K.	N.K.	4.16
Track width (feet) ...	...	...	N.K.	N.K.	N.K.	N.K.	0.78
Tyre size	...	...	N.K.	N.K.	N.K.	N.K.	6.00×20
Engine type	...	...	BMW315	BMW315	BMW319	Maybach HL25	Maybach NL38 TRKM
Cylinders	...	...	6	6	6	4	6
Output (bhp/rpm) ...	...	...	28/2600	28/2600	42/2800	65/2800	83/2400
Gearbox type	...	...	ZF	ZF	ZF	ZF	Demag-Adler
Gears (forward/reverse)	...	...	4/1	4/1	4/1	4/1	6/2
Differential	...	...	Cletrac	Cletrac	Cletrac	Cletrac	Cletrac
Brakes: Steering	...	...	Hydraulic	Hydraulic	Hydraulic	Hydraulic	Hydraulic
Road	...	...	Hydraulic	Hydraulic	Hydraulic	Hydraulic	Hydraulic
Chassis construction	...	...	Hull	Hull	Hull	Hull	Hull
Wheel suspension ...	...	...	Torsion-bar	Torsion-bar	Torsion-bar	None	None
Track suspension ...	...	...	Torsion-bar	Torsion-bar	Torsion-bar	Torsion-bar	Torsion-bar
Bogie wheels per side	...	...	3	4	5	5	5
Idler springing ...	...	...	Torsion-bar	Torsion-bar	Torsion-bar	None	None
Crew	...	...	2	2	2+4	2+6	2+6
Radius of action:							
Road (miles) ...	...	...	N.K.	N.K.	N.K.	200	200
Cross-country (miles)	...	...	N.K.	N.K.	N.K.	85	85
Fuel capacity (galls)	...	...	N.K.	N.K.	N.K.	20–25	20–25
Fording depth (feet) ...	...	...	2	2	2	2	2.3
Grade ability (deg) ...	...	...	20	20	20	20	24
Ground clearance (feet)	...	...	N.K.	N.K.	N.K.	N.K.	1.0
Maximum speed (mph)	...	...	40	40	40	40	40

the vehicle and operated partly as a plough to clear the snow and also as a skid-plate compressing the snow between the tracks and thus providing a clearance for the body and for any following vehicles. It was intended that this should be fitted on leading vehicles of second-line transport and all recovery and reconnaissance vehicles. Thirdly, chains were fitted on every second or third track pad. This had the effect of increasing the ground pressure and breaking up the ice surface. Fourthly, the rubber tyres on the idler wheels were removed and replaced by a steel rim and the rubber pads on the driving sprocket were changed for blade-shaped ice-cutters. This had the effect of preventing ice and snow from building up on the track. Actual operational tests were carried out in Norway and Russia during late 1944.

4: CONVERSION OF ARMOURED HALF-TRACKED VEHICLES TO LOAD CARRIERS

Two cases of the conversion of armoured semi-tracked vehicles for use as load-carriers were noted by the Americans in the European theatre of operations, the armoured bodywork being cut away and replaced by an open lorry type of body. In one case the subject of this operation was the light armoured semi-tracked vehicle Sd.Kfz.250. The other was the medium type Sd.Kfz.251.

The converted vehicles were classified as being roughly equivalent to the 2-ton Maultier vehicle as regards cross-country performance, although the payload was less in both instances. Since these vehicles were far more expensive to produce than the Maultier type, their conversion for load-carrying purposes indicated a severe shortage of the latter.

The converted Sd.Kfz.250 was fitted with a cold-climate cab constructed of a one-inch-thick layer of paper composition sandwiched between quarter-inch wooden panels. The doors were covered with one-eighth inch sheet metal. The two windscreen panels could not be opened. The side windows consisted of two panels— the forward one being pivoted at the top and bottom near the front, to enable it to open, and weatherproofed with rubber packing. (These cabs were produced as an expedient towards the end of the war and were also often fitted to standard lorries; they were termed 'Einheits cabs'.)

A Ford 2-ton 'Maultier' lorry, also used in Europe, was similarly modified for winter operation.

				*Based on D6/based on D7
D7	D8	D7	D7	D7
Demag	Demag	Demag	Demag	Demag
10	Nil	10/1	10/2	10/3
3.40	4.30	4.00	3.83	3.70
4.90	5.80	4.90	4.83	4.50
1.00	1.00	Nil	Nil	Nil
*15.4/15.5	16.70	15.50	15.60	15.50
6.00	6.00	6.00	6.10	6.30
5.78	5.78	5.30	5.30	5.78
5.38	5.38	5.38	5.38	5.38
5.23	5.23	5.23	5.23	5.23
4.48	5.78	4.48	4.48	4.48
0.78	0.78	0.78	0.78	0.78
6.00×20	6.00×20	6.00×20	6.00×20	6.00×20
Maybach HL42 TRKM	Maybach HL42 TRKM	Maybach HL42 TRKM	Maybach HL42 TRKM	Maybach HL42 TRKM
6	6	6	6	6
100/2800	100/2800	100/2800	100/2800	100/2800
Maybach Variorex	Maybach Variorex	Maybach Variorex	Maybach Variorex	Maybach Variorex
7/3	8/3	7/3	7/3	7/3
Cletrac	Cletrac	Cletrac	Cletrac	Cletrac
Hydraulic	Hydraulic	Hydraulic	Hydraulic	Hydraulic
Hydraulic	Hydraulic	Hydraulic	Hydraulic	Hydraulic
Hull	Hull	Hull	Hull	Hull
None	None	None	None	None
Torsion-bar	Torsion-bar	Torsion-bar	Torsion-bar	Torsion-bar
5	6	5	5	5
None	None	None	None	None
2+6	1+7	1+7	1+3	1+1
217	N.K.	217	217	217
93	N.K.	93	93	93
20–25	20–25	20–25	20–25	20–25
2.3	2.3	2.3	2.3	2.3
24	24	24	24	24
1.0	1.0	1.0	1.0	1.0
40	40	5 (operating)	5 (operating)	5 (operating)

3-ton half-track Sd.Kfz.11 series

	HL kl 2	HL kl 3	HL kl 3(H)*	HL kl 4(H)*	HL kl 5	HL kl 6
Original manufacturer	Hansa-Lloyd	Borgward	Borgward	Borgward	Borgward	Borgward
Sd.Kfz. No.	Nil	Nil	Nil	Nil	Nil	11
Weight, unladen (tons)	3.00	5.00	3.50	4.00	5.00	5.65
Weight, laden (tons)	5.00	6.50	6.50	6.50	6.50	7.20
Trailer load (tons) ...	2.50	2.50	Nil	Nil	2.50	3.00
Length, o.a. (feet)	16.15	18.15	16.8	17.15	18.15	18.30
Width, o.a. (feet)	5.70	6.60	6.60	6.60	6.60	6.60
Height, o.a. (feet)	6.42	7.30	N.K.	N.K.	7.30	7.10
Wheel centres (feet)	4.62	5.45	5.45	5.45	5.45	5.45
Track centres (feet)	4.28	5.26	5.26	5.26	5.26	5.26
Ground contact, tracks (feet) ...	3.95	5.94	5.26	5.86	5.94	5.94
Track width (feet)	N.K.	N.K.	N.K.	N.K.	0.93	0.93
Tyre size	N.K.	N.K.	N.K.	N.K.	7.25×20	190×18
Engine type	Borgward L3500	Borgward L3500	Borgward L3500	Borgward	Borgward L3500L	Maybach HL38 TUKR***
Cylinders	6	6	6	6	6	6
Output (nhp/rpm)	70/2600	70/2600	70/2600	100/3000	70/2600	100/2800
Gearbox type	Borgward	ZF	ZF	Borgward	Borgward	Borgward
Gears (forward/reverse)	4/1	5/1	4/1	4/1	4/1	4/1
Differential	Cletrac	Cletrac	Cletrac	Cletrac	Cletrac	Cletrac
Brakes: Steering	Mechanical	Mechanical	Mechanical	Mechanical	Mechanical	Mechanical
Road	Mechanical	Mechanical	Mechanical	Mechanical	Mechanical	Mechanical
Chassis construction	Frame	Frame	Frame	Frame	Frame	Frame
Wheel suspension	Leaf spring	Leaf spring	Leaf spring	Leaf spring	Leaf spring	Leaf spring
Track suspension	Torsion-bar	Torsion-bar	Torsion-bar	Torsion-bar	Torsion-bar	Torsion-bar
Bogie wheels/side	4	4	5	6	6	6
Idler springing	Torsion-bar	Torsion-bar	Torsion-bar	Torsion-bar	Torsion-bar	Torsion-bar
Crew	2+6	2+6	3	3	2+6	2+7
Radius of action:						
Road (miles)	N.K.	N.K.	N.K.	N.K.	172	172
Cross-country (miles) ...	N.K.	N.K.	N.K.	N.K.	94	94
Fuel capacity (galls)	N.K.	N.K.	N.K.	N.K.	24	24
Fording depth (feet)	N.K.	N.K.	N.K.	N.K.	1.6	1.6
Grade ability (deg)	20	20	20	20	24	24
Ground clearance (feet)	N.K.	N.K.	N.K.	N.K.	1.0	1.0
Maximum speed (mph)	31	33	31	31	33	33

5-ton half-track Sd.Kfz.6 series

	BN l 4*	BN l 7	BN l 8	BN 9**	BN 11
Original Manufacturer	Büssing NAG	Büssing NAG	Büssing NAG	Büssing NAG	Büssing NAG
Sd.Kfz. No.	6/1	6 & 6/1	6 & 6/1	6/1	Nil
Weight, unladen (tons) ...	7.30	7.30	7.00	7.50	7.00
Weight, laden (tons) ...	8.80	8.80***	8.50***	9.00	8.40
Trailer load (tons) ...	5.00	5.00	5.00	5.00	5.20
Length, o.a. (feet)	19.8	19.8	20.0	21.0	21.0
Width, o.a. (feet)	7.30	7.30	7.50	7.50	7.50
Height, o.a. (feet)	8.30	8.30	8.20	8.30	8.30
Wheel centres (feet) ...	6.00	6.00	6.00	6.00	6.20
Track centres (feet)	5.60	5.60	5.60	5.60	5.60
Ground contact, tracks (feet) ...	4.20	4.20	6.70	7.26	6.90
Track width (feet)	1.06	1.06	1.06	1.06	1.06
Tyre size	7.50×20	7.50×20	210×18	210×18	210×18
Engine type (Maybach)	NL35	NL38	NL38 TUK****	HL54 TUKRM	HL61
Cylinders	6	6	6	6	6
Output (bhp/rpm)	90/3000	100/3000	100/3000	115/2600	130/2600
Gearbox type	ZF	ZF	ZF	ZF	N.K.
Gears (forward/reverse)	4/1	4/1	4/1	4/1	N.K.

*BN l 5 (Sd.Kfz.6) was identical except for seating capacity (here 15 men).
**BN 9b was identical, but with a modified braking system.

HL kl 6	H 8(H)*	H 7	H kl 6n	H kl 6k	H kl 6s	H kl 6n	H kl 6
Hanomag	Hanomag	Hanomag	Hanomag	Hanomag	Hanomag	Hanomag	Hanomag
11	Nil	Nil	11/1	11/3	11/2	11/4	11/5
5.65	5.67	5.45	5.43	5.43	5.5	5.34	5.40
7.20	8.00	6.50	7.30	7.50	6.7	7.3	7.2
3.00	3.00	3.50	Nil	Nil	Nil	Nil	Nil
18.30	18.30	19.20	23.6	18.2	19.1	18.3	18.3
6.60	6.80	6.80	8.20	6.60	6.6	7.26	6.8
7.10	5.60	7.40	8.90	6.90	7.9	7.69	7.7
5.45	5.45	5.70	5.45	5.45	5.45	5.45	5.45
5.26	5.28	5.30	5.26	5.26	5.26	5.26	5.26
5.94	5.28	6.28	5.94	5.94	5.94	5.94	5.94
0.93	0.93	0.93	0.93	0.93	0.93	0.93	0.93
190×18	190×18	190×18	190×18	190×18	190×18	190×18	190×18
Maybach	Maybach	Maybach	Maybach	Maybach	Maybach	Maybach	Maybach
HL42 TUKRM	HL42 TUKRM**	HL42 TUKRM	HL42 TUKRM	HL42 TUKRM	HL42 TUKRM	HL42 TUKRM	HL42 TUKRM
6	6	6	6	6	6	6	6
100/2800	110/2800	100/2800	100/2800	100/2800	100/2800	100/2800	100/2800
Hanomag	Maybach Variorex	Maybach Variorex	Hanomag	Hanomag	Hanomag	Hanomag	Hanomag
4/1	10/?	7/?	4/1	4/1	4/1	4/1	4/1
Cletrac	Cletrac	Cletrac	Cletrac	Cletrac	Cletrac	Cletrac	Cletrac
Mechanical	Hydraulic	Hydraulic	Mechanical	Mechanical	Mechanical	Mechanical	Mechanical
Mechanical	Pneumatic	Pneumatic	Mechanical	Mechanical	Mechanical	Mechanical	Mechanical
Frame	Frame	Frame	Frame	Frame	Frame	Frame	Frame
Leaf spring	Leaf spring	Leaf spring		Leaf spring	Leaf spring	Leaf spring	Leaf spring
Torsion-bar	Torsion-bar	Torsion-bar		Torsion-bar	Torsion-bar	Torsion-bar	Torsion-bar
6	6	6	6	6	6	6	6
Torsion-bar	None	None	Torsion-bar	Torsion-bar	Torsion-bar	Torsion-bar	Torsion-bar
2+7	2+7	2+7	2	2	2+3	2	2
172	N.K.	N.K.	172	172	172	172	172
94	N.K.	N.K.	94	94	94	94	94
24	N.K.	N.K.	24	24	24	24	24
1.6	N.K.	N.K.	1.6	1.6	1.6	1.6	1.6
24	24	24	24	24	24	24	24
1.0	N.K.	N.K.	1.0	1.0	1.0	1.0	1.0
33	32	32	33	5 (operating)	33	33	33

*Rear engined; was to have been armoured and armed.
**Also fitted with Maybach HL49 TRWS 120hp engine; later with Maybach HL54 TRWS 115hp engine.
***Later with Maybach HL42 TUKRM engine.

	BN 14	DN 17	RN 18	RN 9	BN 11
Differential	Cletrac	Cletrac	Cletrac	Cletrac	Cletrac
Brakes: Steering	Mechanical	Mechanical	Mechanical	Mechanical	N.K.
Road	Pneumatic	Pneumatic	Pneumatic	Pneumatic	N.K.
Chassis construction	Frame	Frame	Frame	Frame	Frame
Wheel suspension	Leaf-spring	Leaf-spring	Leaf-spring	Leaf-spring	Leaf-spring
Track suspension	Leaf-spring	Leaf-spring	Torsion-bar	Torsion-bar	Torsion-bar
Bogie wheels/side	4	4	6	6	6
Idler springing	Torsion-bar	Torsion-bar	Torsion-bar	Nil	Nil
Crew	13	15/13*****	15/13*****	13	12
Radius of action:					
Road (miles)	156	156	156	187	N.K.
Cross-country (miles)	64	64	64	72	N.K.
Fuel capacity (galls)	42	42	42	42	N.K.
Fording depth (feet)	2	2	2	2	2
Grade ability (deg.)	24	24	24	24	24
Ground clearance (feet)	1.2	1.2	1.2	1.2	N.K.
Maximum speed (mph)	31	31	31	31	31

***Varied according to role.
****Also used NL38 TUKRM.
*****Engineer/Artillery bodies.

8-ton half-track Sd.Kfz.7 series

Original Manufacturer	Krauss Maffei	Krauss Maffei	Krauss Maffei	Krauss Maffei	Krauss Maffei	Krauss Maffei
Sd.Kfz. No.	7	7	7	7	Nil	7/6
Weight, unladen (tons)	9.50	8.90	8.90	9.75	9.40	9.75
Weight, laden (tons)	11.00	10.74	10.74	11.55	10.90	11.40
Trailer load (tons)	8.00	8.00	8.00	8.00	8.00	8.00
Length, o.a. (feet)	22.0	22.0	22.0	22.6	22.6	24.8
Width, o.a. (feet)	7.75	7.75	7.75	7.91	7.91	7.91
Height, o.a. (feet)	9.10	8.10	9.10	8.65	N.K.	9.10
Wheel centres (feet)	6.40	6.40	6.40	6.60	6.35	6.60
Track centres (feet)	5.78	5.78	5.78	5.94	5.94	5.94
Ground contact, tracks (feet)	4.63	4.63	4.63	7.70	7.60	7.70
Track width (feet)	1.18	1.18	1.18	1.18	1.18	1.18
Tyre size	7.50×20	7.50×20	7.50×20	9.75×20	9.75×20	9.75×20
Engine type (Maybach)	HL52 TU*	HL57 TU	HL62 TUK***	HL62 TUK***	HL80	HL62 TUK
Cylinders	6	6	6	6	6	6
Output (bhp/rpm)	120/2600	130/2600	140/2600	140/2600	160/2600	140/2600
Gearbox type	ZF	ZF	ZF	ZF	N.K.	ZF
Gears (forward/reverse)	4/1	4/1	4/1	4/1	N.K.	4/1
Differential	Cletrac	Cletrac	Cletrac	Cletrac	Cletrac	Cletrac
Brakes: Steering	Mechanical	Mechanical	Mechanical	Mechanical	Mechanical	Mechanical
Road	Pneumatic	Pneumatic	Pneumatic	Pneumatic	N.K.	Pneumatic
Chassis construction	Frame	Frame	Frame	Frame	Frame	Frame
Wheel suspension	Leaf-spring	Leaf-spring	Leaf-spring	Leaf-spring	Leaf-spring	Leaf-spring
Track suspension	Leaf-spring	Leaf-spring	Leaf-spring	Leaf-spring**	Torsion-bar	Leaf-spring**
Bogie wheels/side	4	4	4	6	6	6
Idler springing	Coil-spring	Torsion-bar	Torsion-bar	Torsion-bar	None	Torsion-bar
Crew	12	12	12	12	12	13
Radius of action:						
Road (miles)	156	156	156	156	N.K.	156
Cross-country (miles)	63	63	63	63	N.K.	63
Fuel capacity (galls)	47	47	47	47	N.K.	47
Fording depth (feet)	2	2	2	2	2	2
Grade ability (deg.)	24	24	24	24	N.K.	24
Ground clearance (feet)	1.3	1.3	1.3	1.3	N.K.	1.3
Maximum speed (mph)	31	31	31	31	50	31

*Later with 130hp HL57 engine.   **Later torsion-bar.   ***Also made by Nordbau under licence.

12-ton half-track Sd.Kfz.8 series

	DB s 7	DB s 8	DB s 9	DB s 10	DB 11
Original Manufacturer	Daimler-Benz	Daimler-Benz	Daimler-Benz	Daimler-Benz	Daimler-Benz
Sd.Kfz. No.	8	8	8	8	Nil
Weight, unladen (tons)	12.60	12.50	13.40	12.15	N.K.
Weight, laden (tons)	14.40	15.00	14.70	14.70	14.00
Trailer load (tons)	12.00	12.00	12.00	12.00	12.00
Length, o.a. (feet)	22.50	23.40	23.40	24.18	24.80
Width, o.a. (feet)	7.75	7.91	7.91	8.25	8.31
Height, o.a. (feet)	7.26	9.25	9.25	9.15	N.K.
Wheel centres (feet)	6.28	6.28	6.28	6.93	6.65
Track centres (feet)	6.12	6.28	6.28	6.28	6.28
Ground contact, tracks (feet)	7.10	8.25	8.25	8.25	8.25
Track width (feet)	1.32	1.32	1.32	1.32	1.32
Tyre size	9.00×20	11.25×20	11.25×20	11.25×20	11.25×20
Engine type	DSO8	DSO8	Maybach HL85 TUKRM*	Maybach HL85 TUKRM*	Maybach HL95
Cylinders	V12	V12	V12	V12	V12
Output (bhp/rpm)	200/3200	200/3200	185/2600	185/2600	200/2500
Gearbox type	ZF	ZF	ZF	ZF	N.K.
Gears (forward/reverse)	4/1	4/1	4/1	4/1	N.K.
Differential	Cletrac	Cletrac	Cletrac	Cletrac	Cletrac
Brakes: Steering	Mechanical	Mechanical	Hydraulic	Hydraulic**	N.K.
Road	Pneumatic	Pneumatic	Pneumatic	Pneumatic	N.K.
Chassis construction	Frame	Frame	Frame	Frame	Frame
Wheel suspension	Leaf-spring	Leaf-spring	Leaf-spring	Leaf-spring	Leaf-spring
Track suspension	Leaf-spring	Leaf-spring	Leaf-spring	Torsion-bar	Torsion-bar
Bogie wheels/side	5	6	6	6	6
Idler springing	Leaf-spring	Torsion-bar	Torsion-bar	None	None
Crew	13	13	13	13	13
Radius of action:					
Road (miles)	156	156	156	156	N.K.
Cross-country (miles)	62	62	62	62	N.K.
Fuel capacity (galls)	55	55	55	55	N.K.
Fording depth (feet)	2	2	2	2	2
Grade ability (deg.)	24	24	24	24	24
Ground clearance (feet)	1.32	1.32	1.32	1.32	N.K.
Maximum speed (mph)	31	31	31	31	50

*Originally used DSO8 engine.   **Steering brakes originally mechanical.

18-ton half-track Sd.Kfz.9 series

	FM gr 1	F2	F3	F4
Original Manufacturer	Famo	Famo	Famo	Famo
Sd.Kfz. No.	Nil	Nil	9	Nil
Weight, unladen (tons)	15.13	15.13	15.13	N.K.
Weight, laden (tons)	18.00	18.00	18.00	18.00
Trailer load (tons)	18.00	18.00	18.00	18.00
Length, o.a. (feet)	27.21	27.21	27.21	26.10
Width, o.a. (feet)	8.59	8.59	8.59	8.59
Height, o.a. (feet)	9.40	9.40	9.40	N.K.
Wheel centres (feet)	6.94	6.94	6.94	6.94
Track centres (feet)	6.60	6.60	6.60	6.60
Ground contact, tracks (feet)	9.40	9.40	9.40	9.40
Track width (feet)	1.45	1.45	1.45	1.45
Tyre size	12.75×20	12.75×20	12.75×20	N.K.
Engine type (Maybach)	HL98 TUK	HL98 TUK	HL108 TUKRM	HL 116
Cylinders	V12	V12	V12	V12
Output (bhp/rpm)	230/2600	230/2600	250/2600	260/2400
Gearbox type	ZF	ZF	ZF	N.K.
Gears (forward/reverse)	4/1	4/1	4/1	N.K.
Differential	Cletrac	Cletrac	Cletrac	Cletrac
Brakes: Steering	Mechanical	Mechanical	Mechanical	N.K.
Road	Pneumatic	Pneumatic	Pneumatic	N.K.
Chassis construction	Frame	Frame	Frame	Frame
Wheel suspension	Leaf-spring	Leaf-spring	Leaf-spring	Leaf-spring
Track suspension	Torsion-bar	Torsion-bar	Torsion-bar	Torsion-bar
Bogie wheels/side	6	6	6	6
Idler springing	Torsion-bar	None	None	None
Crew	9	9	9	9
Radius of action:				
Road (miles)	N.K.	161	161	N.K.
Cross-country (miles)	N.K.	62	62	N.K.
Fuel capacity (galls)	N.K.	64	64	N.K.
Fording depth (feet)	2.6	2.6	2.6	2.6
Grade ability (deg.)	24	24	24	24
Ground clearance (feet)	N.K.	1.45	1.45	N.K.
Maximum speed (mph)	N.K.	31	31	49

Adler standardised half-track range

	A1	A2	A3	A3F
Original Manufacturer	Adler	Adler	Adler	Adler
Sd.Kfz. No.	None	None	None	None
Weight, unladen (tons)	2.60	2.00	2.25	2.78
Weight, laden (tons)	3.00	2.60	3.45	3.28
Trailer load (tons)	0.45	0.68	0.90	1.00
Length, o.a. (feet)	12.20	12.50	12.50	13.10
Width, o.a. (feet)	5.60	5.45	5.95	6.26
Height, o.a. (feet)	4.95	5.35	5.95	6.10
Wheel centres (feet)	4.78	4.55	4.86	4.88
Track centres (feet)	4.62	4.52	4.95	4.95
Ground contact, tracks (feet)	2.24	3.10	3.10	3.33
Track width (feet)	0.78	0.78	0.78	0.78
Tyre size	6.00×20	6.00×20	6.00×20	6.00×20
Engine type	Maybach HL25	Maybach HL28	Maybach HL25	Maybach HL28
Cylinders	4	4	4	4
Output (bhp/rpm)	65/3000	78/3000	65/3000	78/3000
Gearbox type	Adler	Adler	Adler	Adler
Gears (forward/reverse)	6/1	6/1	6/1	6/1
Differential	Cletrac	Cletrac	Cletrac	Cletrac
Brakes: Steering	Hydraulic	Hydraulic	Hydraulic	Hydraulic
Road	Hydraulic	Hydraulic	Hydraulic	Hydraulic
Chassis construction	Hull	Hull	Hull	Hull
Wheel suspension	Leaf-spring	Leaf-spring	Leaf-spring	Leaf-spring
Track suspension	Rubber bush	Torsion-bar	Torsion-bar	Torsion-bar
Bogie wheels/side	3*	4	4	4
Idler springing	None	None	None	None
Crew	5	6	6	6
Radius of action:				
Road (miles)	200	200	200	200
Cross-country (miles)	85	85	85	85
Fuel capacity (galls)	20–25	20–25	20–25	20–25
Fording depth (feet)	2	2	2	2
Grade ability (deg.)	20	20	20	20
Ground clearance (feet)	1.0	1.0	1.0	1.0
Maximum speed (mph)	40	40	40	46

*Later changed to 4.

HK standardised half-track range

	HK101*	HK102***	HK301	HK305
Original Manufacturer	NSU	NSU	Adler	Adler
Sd.Kfz. No.	2**	Nil	Nil	Nil
Weight, unladen (tons)	1.24	1.50	2.30	5.77
Weight, laden (tons)	1.56	2.25	3.50	8.21
Trailer load (tons)	0.45	0.45	0.9–1.6	3.00
Length, o.a. (feet)	9.91	11.38	12.90	18.10
Width, o.a. (feet)	3.30	3.80	6.14	7.65
Height, o.a. (feet)	3.96	4.29	6.05	6.92
Wheel centres (feet)	single	single	5.11	5.86
Track centres (feet)	2.70	2.84	4.95	6.04
Ground contact, tracks (feet) ...	2.71	3.96	3.31	5.05
Track width (feet)	0.56	0.56	0.78	0.78
Tyre size	3.50×19	3.50×19	6.00×20	6.00×20
Engine type	Opel Olympia	Stump K20	Maybach HL30	Maybach HL42
Cylinders	4	4	4	6
Output (bhp/rpm)	37/3400	65/3500	95/3000	100/2800
Gearbox type	NSU	NSU	Adler	Maybach-Olvar
Gears (forward/reverse)	3/1	3/1	6/1	8/2
Differential	Cletrac	Epicyclic	Cletrac	Cletrac
Brakes: Steering	Mechanical	Hydraulic	Hydraulic	Pneumatic
Road	Mechanical	N.K.	Mechanical	Pneumatic
Chassis construction	Hull	Hull	Hull	Hull
Wheel suspension	Spiral-springs	Spiral-springs	Leaf-spring	Torsion-bar
Track suspension	Torsion-bar	Torsion-bar	Torsion-bar	Torsion-bar
Bogie wheels/side	4	4	4	4
Idler springing	None	None	None	None
Crew	3	6	8	8
Radius of action:				
Road (miles)	156	156	200	200
Cross-country (miles) ...	94	94	85	85
Fuel capacity (galls)	8.4	8.4	20–25	20–25
Fording depth (feet)	2	2	2	2
Grade ability (deg.)	24	24	20	20
Ground clearance (feet)	0.75	0.75	1.0	1.0
Maximum speed (mph)	50	50	46	34

*Kleines Ketten Kraftrad.
**Originally V.Kfz.620.

The Wehrmacht Schleppers

	Le.WS (1st & 2nd mods.)	Le.WS (3rd mod.)	S.WS
Original Manufacturer	Adler	Adler	Büssing NAG
Sd.Kfz. No.	Nil	Nil	Nil
Weight, unladen (tons)	5.90	5.77	9.50
Weight, laden (tons)	6.90	8.21	13.50*
Trailer load (tons)	3.00	3.00	8.00
Length, o.a. (feet)	17.18	18.10	22.0
Width, o.a. (feet)	7.00	7.65	8.25
Height, o.a. (feet)	6.60	6.92	9.35
Wheel centres (feet)	5.94	5.86	6.93
Track centres (feet)	6.00	6.04	6.44
Ground contact, tracks (feet) ...	4.45	5.05	6.74
Track width (feet)	0.78	0.78	1.64
Tyre size	6.00×20	6.00×20	210×18
Engine type	Maybach HL30	Maybach HL42	Maybach HL61**
Cylinders	4	6	6
Output (bhp/rpm)	95/3000	100/2800	100/3000
Gearbox type	ZF-Adler	ZF-Adler	ZF
Gears (forward/reverse)	4/2	4/2	4/2

*Armoured-cab weighed 14 tons (fully laden).

HK601	HK605****	HK901	HK904	HK905	HK1601
Hanomag	Demag	Krauss-Maffei	Krauss-Maffei	Krauss-Maffei	Daimler-Benz
Nil	Nil	Nil	Nil	Nil	Nil
4.80	5.30	10.00	10.00	10.00	14.20
6.30	6.80	11.80	11.80	11.80	16.20
4.50	4.50	8.00	8.00	8.00	16.00
18.30	18.40	21.20	21.20	21.20	25.60
6.94	6.94	7.60	7.60	7.60	8.59
6.60	6.11	N.K.	N.K.	N.K.	7.75
5.60	5.60	6.26	6.26	6.26	6.70
5.35	5.45	5.94	5.94	5.94	6.70
5.94	6.54	7.00	7.00	7.00	8.58
N.K.	N.K.	1.18	1.18	1.18	1.32
N.K.	N.K.	9.75×20	9.75×20	9.75×20	11.25×20
Maybach HL45Z	Maybach HL50	Maybach HL45Z	Maybach HL66	Maybach HL66	Maybach HL116*****
6	6	6	6	6	6
120/3000	170/3800	120/3000	180/3000	180/3000	250/2600
Hanomag-Maybach	Maybach-Olvar	Maybach	Maybach	Olvar	ZF
8/2	8/2	8/2	8/2	8/2	6/1
Cletrac	Cletrac	Cletrac	Cletrac	Cletrac	Cletrac
Hydraulic	Pneumatic	Mechanical	Mechanical	Mechanical	Hydraulic
Pneumatic	Pneumatic	Pneumatic	Pneumatic	Pneumatic	Pneumatic
Hull	Hull	Frame	Frame	Frame	Frame
Leaf-spring	Leaf-spring	Leaf-spring	Leaf-spring	Leaf-spring	Leaf-spring
Torsion-bar	Torsion-bar	Torsion-bar	Torsion-bar	Torsion-bar	Torsion-bar
6	6	6	6	6	6
None	None	None	None	None	None
8	8	12	12	12	13
N.K.	N.K.	156	156	156	156
N.K.	N.K.	63	63	63	63
N.K.	N.K.	47	47	47	55
2	2	2	2	2	2
24	24	24	24	24	24
N.K.	N.K.	1.30	1.30	1.30	1.32
47	48	48	48	48	42

***Grosses Ketten Kraftrad
****Partially armoured.
*****Intended to have 12 cylinder Maybach 10 320hp engine.

	Le.WS (1st & 2nd mods.)	Le.WS (3rd mod.)	S.WS
Differential	Cletrac	Cletrac	Cletrac
Brakes: Steering	Pneumatic	Pneumatic	Pneumatic
Road	Pneumatic	Pneumatic	Pneumatic
Chassis construction	Hull	Hull	Frame
Wheel suspension	Leaf-spring	Torsion-bar	Leaf-spring
Track suspension	Torsion-bar	Torsion-bar	Torsion-bar
Bogie wheels/side	4	4	5
Idler springing	None	None	None
Crew	8	8	2+10
Radius of action:			
Road (miles)	200	200	187
Cross-country (miles)	85	85	63
Fuel capacity (galls)	20–25	20–25	60
Fording depth (feet)	2	2	3.25
Grade ability (deg.)	20	20	24
Ground clearance (feet)	1.0	1.0	1.6
Maximum speed (mph)	14.4	24	17

**Originally HL42 TRKMS 6-cylinder engine developing 100bhp at 3,000 rpm.

Maultiers

	3.6–36S/SSM	V3000S/SSM	S3000/SSM	L4500R
Original Manufacturer	Opel	Ford	Klöckner-Humboldt-Deutz	Mercedes-Benz
Sd.Kfz. No.	3a	3b	3c	3/5*
Weight, unladen (tons)	3.93	3.86	4.65	7.74
Weight, laden (tons)	5.93	5.86	6.65	12.70
Trailer load (tons)	3.00	2.00	3.00	5.00
Length, o.a. (feet)	19.98	20.82	20.10	26.0
Width, o.a. (feet)	7.52	7.41	7.32	7.80
Height, o.a. (feet)	8.95	9.15	9.24	9.90
Wheel centres (feet)	5.10	5.45	5.41	6.14
Track centres (feet)	5.91	5.91	5.86	5.94
Ground contact, tracks (feet)	6.08	6.08	6.08	7.93
Track width (feet)	0.83**	0.83**	0.83**	0.83**
Tyre size	7.25×20	7.25×20	7.25×20	7.25×20
Engine type	Opel ohv (petrol)	Ford side-valve (petrol)	KH–D (diesel)	Mercedes-Benz (diesel)
Cylinders	6	V-8	4	6
Output (bhp/rpm)	68/3000	83/3000	70/3000	112/2250
Gearbox type	Opel	Ford	ZF	ZF
Gears (forward/reverse)	5	5	5	5
Differential	Bevel-pinion	Bevel-pinion	Bevel-pinion	Bevel-pinion
Brakes: Steering	Mechanical	Mechanical	Mechanical	Mechanical
Road	Hydraulic	Hydraulic	Hydraulic	Hydraulic
Chassis construction	Frame	Frame	Frame	Frame
Wheel suspension	Leaf-spring	Leaf-spring	Leaf-spring	Leaf-spring
Track suspension	Spiral-spring	Spiral-spring	Spiral-spring	Spiral-spring
Bogie wheels/side	4	4	4	5
Idler springing	None	None	None	None
Crew	2+15	2+15	2+15	2+15
Radius of action:				
Road (miles)	100	100	100	100
Cross-country (miles)	48	48	48	48
Fuel capacity (galls)	16	16	16	16
Fording depth (feet)	2	2	2	2
Grade ability (deg.)	24	24	24	24
Ground clearance (feet)	1.0	1.0	1.0	1.0
Maximum speed (mph)	24	25	25	23

*Originally Sd.Kfz.4.

**0.92ft tracks for snow.